Gary Nederveld with Erica Chung

Faith & Finances

Helping People Manage Their Money

CRC Publications, Grand Rapids, Michigan

MidAmerica Leadership Foundation, Chicago, Illinois

We welcome your comments. Call us at 1-800-333-8300 or email us at editors@crcpublications.org.

Library of Congress Cataloging-in-Publication Data
Nederveld, Gary, 1944-
    Faith & finances: helping people manage their money / Gary Nederveld with Erica Chung.
        p.   cm.
    Includes bibliographical references.
    ISBN 1-56212-570-2
    1. Wealth—Religious aspects—Christianity. 2. Stewardship, Christian.
3. Finance, Personal—Religious aspects—Christianity. 4. Money—Religious aspects—Christianity. I. Title: Faith and finances. II. Chung, Erica, 1976-
III. Title.

BR115.W4 N44 2000
  241'.68—dc21

                                                                    00-058543

10 9 8 7 6 5 4 3 2 1

Acknowledgments

This course would not have been possible without the cooperative efforts of many. Most of the charm—such as it is—and much of the substance of this course were brought by Erica Chung, who has been a joy to work with. As this course is being produced, Erica is leaving MidAmerica Leadership Foundation to direct the Chinatown Chamber of Commerce in Chicago.

Special acknowledgment goes to Rhonda Hardy of the Universtiy of Ilinois Cooperative Extension Service, Kevin Davy now of South Shore Bank, and Lyman Howell of the Christian Reformed World Relief Committee for assistance in developing this curriculum. Rev. Sarah Jo Sarchet, Stewardship Minister at Fourth Presbyterian Church in Chicago, offered lots of good advice and pilot tested a number of modules. Ruth Wuorenma, President, Neighborhood Capital Company, LLC, provided valuable content for the home ownership module. Scott Johnson, friend and former colleague who is now studying business and culture in a PhD program at the University of Minnesota, offered suggestions and provided content for the investing module.

We are very grateful to the participants who helped us pilot test this program and who taught us much about financial literacy. They kept our focus on the real issues and barriers to saving and investing.

Thanks also goes to Marlene Brands, Associate Curriculum Editor at CRC Publications, for her major contributions to the final product and her gracious suggestions and guidance. Her background in the area of family resource management was an asset.

Finally, I want to publicly recognize Pat Nederveld, my life companion, who has been a model for managing our family's resources, focusing on what is important now, in the future, and for eternity.

—Gary Nederveld

Contents

Prologue

The journey of developing sound money management skills is a necessary one for all people regardless of their present financial status. This journey involves opportunities, obstacles, and challenges. We recognize that the rules on the journey are not all fair; some of the old suggestions we've followed haven't been very helpful. Some of the travelers enjoy great advantages; some, through no fault of their own, experience hardship.

Churches and other ministries, living together in community, can play a vital role in helping adults on their *faith-based* money management journey. We as a Christian community must do what we can to seek justice and more equal opportunity for all.

We have come to the conclusion that a new approach is needed to solve the problem of financial distress and materialism. In both policy and practice, this approach must encourage more development of assets in the individual, the family, and the community with less emphasis on consumption. We are convinced that individuals who take steps to improve their own situation will contribute to improved communities, and improved communities will create conditions in which more individuals will find success on their journey.

We value the stories of people who have escaped materialism and poverty by force of their determined character or with the assistance of family and community. But what is needed today is a strategy that brings real progress to groups or communities of people. Where will the energy come from to drive this new direction? We believe that the source of the energy needed in an exhausted society is our faith. *Real financial health is a faith-community issue.* Scripture tells us so.

Jesus gave these instructions to the rich young man seeking eternal life: "Go, sell everything you have and give to the poor" (Mark 10:21). Jesus makes clear to us that wealth can stand in the way of our becoming disciples. The *love* of wealth was this seeker's downfall. It kept him outside of the kingdom. The disciples were shocked. But Jesus told them, "It is easier for a camel to go through the eye of a needle than for [the rich] to enter the kingdom of God" (v. 25).

Peter, perhaps feeling a little defensive and concerned about the application of this Scripture to himself, quickly reminded Jesus that he and the disciples had left all for him (v. 28). So what could they expect? They must have rejoiced when they heard that they would receive a return of a hundred times what they gave up in this present age—and eternal life! But did the disciples under-

Notepad

For an excellent treatment of the teachings of Scripture on wealth and poverty, we suggest Craig L. Blomberg's book *Neither Poverty Nor Riches,* (Wm. B. Eerdmans, 1999). Ron Sider, author of the best-selling *Rich Christians in an Age of Hunger* (Word, 1997), offers a holistic, biblical approach for caring about the poor in his book *Just Generosity: A New Vision for Overcoming Poverty in America* (Baker Books, 1999). Susan van Lopik's *Just Generosity: A Study and Action Guide* (Evangelicals for Social Action, Christian Reformed World Relief Committee, CRC Publications, 1999) is a helpful resource for small group discussion of Sider's book. In his book *Justice, Not Just Us,* (Public Justice Resource Centre, 1999), political veteran Gerald Vande Zande presents a faith perspecitve on public justice concerns facing Canadians, including child poverty and worsening economic inequity.

stand that the brothers and sisters, mothers and children, homes and fields are what we receive when we create a community of faith that shares, especially with the poor and needy? That's the understanding we're challenged to develop on our faith-based money management journey.

—Gary Nederveld, Executive Director, MidAmerica Leadership Foundation

And let us consider how we may spur one another on toward love and good deeds . . . let us encourage one another—and all the more as you see the Day approaching.

—Hebrews 10:24-25

Getting Started:
An Introduction to the Program

This section of the program guide is designed to introduce leaders to the *Faith and Finances* program.

Getting Started:
An Introduction to the Program

From a financial perspective, the church community today probably represents society as a whole; polarization between the rich and poor exists in the pew as much as in the marketplace. Yet the church is in a unique position to equalize the two groups by fostering a faith-based approach to money management.

This *Faith and Finances* program is designed to help deacons and other leaders in the church work specifically with those in the church and community who are struggling to manage their money. It provides a biblical foundation for stewardship, offers participants important information about our economic system, and teaches participants practical skills for changing their financial practices that will empower them to become part of a giving faith community.

Depending on the social, cultural, and economic makeup of a church community, participants might be single parents struggling to make ends meet, blue-collar or white-collar workers coping with company downsizing, people of various ethnic origins eking out an existence in the core cities, farmers tending the red clay hills of Georgia or the debt-ridden farms of Iowa, migrant workers coming from anywhere in North America, or First Nations or Native American people subsisting on reservations. They are unique people faced with both the common and the extraordinary problems stemming from economic hard times, often lacking knowledge about money management and opportunities to participate in the economic system.

Understanding the Program

This program guide is intended for use by deacons and other leaders in a group setting or in a one-to-one mentoring situation. It provides background information as well as helpful tools for working with participants over a period of approximately ten weeks.

Program Modules

The guide is organized into four program modules. Module One develops the biblical basis for stewardship and sound money management. Module Two gives participants basic knowledge about our market-based economy and its impact on their lives, and Module Three encourages participants to develop behaviors that will give them a more financially secure future. Module Four, building on the concept of stewardship introduced in Module One, encourages the *practice* of stewardship.

HELP LINE

Ideally, we assume that you will organize your program in the order given in this guide. However, we know that participant groups can vary widely in terms of needs, financial and life experiences, and where they are spiritually. To respond to some situations you might encounter, we've suggested alternative ways to organize the material in this guide (see "Alternative Program Plans," pp. 16-18).

Here is an overview of the four program modules with their individual sessions as presented in this guide:

- Module One: Setting the Course
  Session 1: Stewardship
  Session 2: Money and Me

- Module Two: Building Knowledge
  Session 1: Market Economics
  Session 2: Materialism vs. Values

- Module Three: Changing Behavior
  Session 1: Thrifty Living
  Session 2: Risk Management
  Session 3: Debt Management
  Session 4: Home Ownership
  Session 5: Investing

- Module Four: Giving Back

HELP LINE

In Module One, Session 1, we've suggested that you share an overview of the program with the participants (see p. 23). We've included a transparency master of this information in a more visual format in the reproducible materials section of this guide (see *Faith and Finances:* A Brief Overview," p. 130).

Session Plans

Session plans provide background information for leaders and a step-by-step plan for presenting the concepts to participants during a one-and-one-half to two-hour time period. Each session plan is organized around these key components:

- Session Focus (key concept statement)
- Session Goals (what participants will be helped to do)
- Session Brief (quick overview of the session plan)
- For the Leader (background information about the session topic)
- Building Community (ice-breaker and introductory ideas)
- Spiritual Reflection (biblical references and Scriptural perspective)
- Application Activities (ideas to help participants meet the session goals and apply the information to their own situations)
- Follow-up Activity (suggestions to encourage independent learning)
- Wrap-up (closing ideas)
- Optional Activities (ideas to extend the session or to tailor activities to a particular need)

Some of the content included in the "For the Leader" sections may also be valuable for the participants to know. We have highlighted this information on transparency masters included in the reproducible materials section in the back of this program guide. You may wish to make a transparency to use with the group or a photocopy for each participant. Each transparency is referred to by title and page number in the session plan.

Throughout the session plans, we've used shaded or lined boxes to call attention to important information. The **Notepad** sidebars provide additional notes (statistics, definitions, scenarios, and so on) for the leader—the leader may or may not share this information with group members. The **Help Line** boxes give helpful suggestions for how to present a concept or activity to the group or provide brief background information for discussion.

Handouts for each session are included in the reproducible materials section in the back of this program guide; they may be photocopied for distribution to participants. Each handout is referred to by title and page number in the session plan.

The Appendix

The Appendix contains more detailed information about particular concepts covered in the session plans. This information is referred to by title and page number in the session plans.

Organizing the Program

This program is designed to be used with a group in a somewhat structured setting or with individuals in a more informal mentoring situation. We encourage you to use the group setting whenever possible so that group members can encourage and support each other, give suggestions, share resources, and increase the impact of the program. Or you may want to consider a combination of large or small group sessions along with some mentoring sessions (or use this combination within each session).

Leadership Roles

The way you set up the program will determine the kind of leadership needed. If you are using this program in a group setting, we recommend that you identify the following three roles (a person may serve in more than one of these roles):

- Facilitator
  The facilitator, along with available support staff, is responsible for putting the program together (promoting, scheduling, arranging for meeting space, and so on) and for organizing the resources (handouts, speakers, audio-visual equipment, refreshments, and so on) needed to carry out the session plans. During the group session, the facilitator may serve as organizer, presenter, motivator, liaison—all part of being a change agent. He or she may form follow-up sessions such as solidarity groups or circles of accountability to encourage members to give support to each other.

- Presenter
  The presenter may be the facilitator or a guest expert invited to lead all or part of a session. For example, facilitators may wish to invite someone with

expertise in investing to present the last session in Module Three. (It's important that the facilitator communicate to the invited guest the specific purpose and format of the session and the needs of the participants.)

- Mentors

  Mentors support, encourage, and guide participants through the steps on their faith-based money management journey. Like a coach, mentors focus on the "how to," helping participants, usually one-on-one, understand new concepts and develop new money management skills. Mentors need not be financial experts—developing a supportive relationship with the participant is the most important part of their role. Mentoring is especially valuable to someone changing a behavior pattern or assuming new responsibility and is one of the key factors in this program's success.

HELP LINE

Mentoring becomes critical when working with adults who read at very low levels or not at all. Developers of OPEN DOOR BOOKS, a literacy program for adults who are illiterate or who are learning English as a second language, find that

> *Even though people are becoming more sensitive to adults with reading difficulties, many of those who need assistance are still ashamed to reveal their problem and ask for help. In fact, these adults may take elaborate measures to conceal their lack of reading skills. The church [and community agencies] can be especially supportive in this situation by assisting members with reading difficulties to find tutoring help and by making sure that they are not excluded from the . . . activities that require reading.*

> —Adapted from *Opening Minds, Changing Lives*, Program Packet,
> © OPEN DOOR MINISTRIES/CRC Publications, 1999, p. 4.

We've offered some tips on how to identify participants who can't read and information about reading levels of selected versions of the Bible in the Appendix (see "Language as Ministry," p. 180).

Developing Sensitivity

Those in leadership roles on this faith-based money management journey must be prepared to learn and change along with the participants. Scripture gives us a convincing illustration of that in Acts 10 when Peter was asked to go to the house of Cornelius, a Gentile. While Peter was reluctant to visit the home of a Gentile, Cornelius was eager and ready to listen to what God had to say to him through Peter. After Cornelius and his household heard the message of salvation, the Holy Spirit was poured out "even on the Gentiles" (Acts 10:45). God changed Peter's thinking and the destiny of the church. Peter recognized that God does not show favoritism but accepts all people who accept the good news of Jesus Christ.

Scripture also reminds us not to show favoritism because of one's wealth or fine clothing (James 2:1-4). Most of us have a tendency to associate with and reach out to those who are like us. Even though many of us do not consider ourselves wealthy, we likely are part of the one-fifth of the world's population that has disproportionate access to the world's resources and opportunities. We can afford luxuries in addition to the essentials, we have choices about the work we do, and we can build up wealth for the future.

So we must make a concerted effort to embrace the remaining four-fifths of the world's population. The more than one billion people who comprise the "bottom" fifth of the world's population struggle for survival at the edge of subsistence, lacking the most basic requirements for life. They travel by foot, eat an inadequate diet, drink contaminated water, and live in open or rudimentary shelters. The middle three-fifths of the world's population normally have their basic needs met but live on the edge of disaster with periodic times of shortage.

Regardless of the disparity that may exist between the leaders of your program and those who participate, it's important to "show special attention" and provide a "good seat" for each person to whom you minister. Then you will avoid having "discriminated among yourselves and become judges with evil thoughts," as James cautions (2:3-4).

HELP LINE

Some sectors of our North American population face greater economic hardship than others due to factors such as race, culture, and gender. For example,

- In 1995, according to the Survey of Consumer Finances, the median figure for assets owned by Caucasian families was $73,000 compared to $16,500 for families of color—a gap of more than four to one (Julianne Malveaux, "Banking on Us: The State of Black Wealth," *Essence*, October, 1998).
- According to a recent study conducted for the American Association of Retired Persons (AARP), "Asian-Americans, Hispanics, and African-Americans are much more likely than whites to be providing financial assistance to parents or in-laws. This reflects both economic need—minority group retirees tend to be poorer than whites—and tradition" (Susan Jacoby, "The Allure of Money," *Modern Maturity*, July-August, 2000, p. 39).
- "Divorced or separated women were twice as likely as divorced or separated men—and more than two and a half times as likely as married women—to rate themselves 'below average' financially. And this disparity carries over into retirement. Less than 40 percent of divorced or separated female retirees, compared with 64 percent of divorced or separated men, said they have enough money to live comfortably" (Jacoby, p. 37).

In addition to the factors illustrated above, participants' religious beliefs may impact their socio-economic lifestyle and decisions. For example, those of the Muslim faith believe that women should stay at home with small children, elderly parents should be cared for at home, and interest should not be charged by lenders.

Choice of occupation may be another factor. Over the past two decades, many farm families across North America have experienced economic hardship due to a number of environmental and economic stressors. Downsizing and mergers have affected the lives of both blue-collar and white-collar workers.

Your group may reflect these and other factors that influence their receptiveness to learning more about managing their money. Information must be presented in a way that is relevant and respectful. In order to do this well, those in leadership roles must be aware of and modest about their own worldview and how these views differ from those of the participants.

A Word of Encouragement

This program, designed to help people on their journey toward sound financial management, is based on the experiences of participants across the globe. Many steps were borrowed from successful approaches used in development programs in Asia, Africa, and Latin America. These programs encourage community and self-support by forming cohesive groups and networks to meet social and economic as well as spiritual and educational needs. They organize the community, expand the leadership base, and offer practical help such as group savings and investment, credit, job leads, and shared child care.

The MidAmerica Leadership Foundation, as it was developing the *Faith and Finances* program, found that these ideas that worked overseas worked in North America too. We trust you'll be encouraged by these comments from residents of the Cabrini housing project in Chicago who participated in the pilot testing of this program:

- "This program has really helped me to think about saving. I looked at my life and thought about what I could start giving up. I realized I was spending $60-$80 a month to upkeep my nails, so I gave that up. Now they're natural, and they look just fine!"
- "I don't buy French fries anymore. I buy the large bags of potatoes at the store."
- "This program gives me the motivation to save and think in the long-term. I'm building for the future."
- "I've never thought of getting a bank account before. What's the point if you're going to put something in and then take it right back out?"

Step-by-step, these residents of Chicago are on their faith-based financial management journey. People in your church and community are ready to take the same first step—journey with them, trusting God to bless your walk together.

Let us not become weary in doing good, for at the proper time we will reap a harvest if we do not give up. Therefore, as we have opportunity, let us do good to all people, especially to those who belong to the family of believers.

—Galatians 6:9-10

Alternative Program Plans

These alternative program plans are only a guideline to help you adapt *Faith and Finances* to the spiritual maturity level of participants in your group, to their individual financial and life experiences, and to their specific needs for information. We encourage you to make further changes as you become more sensitive to the variety of situations participants bring to this program.

HELP LINE

Stewardship. You may be using this program as part of your side-door ministry to people in your community who have no direct connection to your church or to any Christian church. If so, *biblical and faith-based stewardship* may be a very new concept to them. You will need to decide how to present the Spiritual Reflection activity in each session and consider the changes we've suggested below for Module One. It might be best to wait to emphasize stewardship until the end of your program, using Module Four.

Module One/Session 1: Stewardship (pp. 20-28)

Getting Started (p. 22)
✔ Omit Step 1 (the transparency "Biblical Guidelines for Stewardship" can be used in Module Four).

A Steward Is . . . (p. 25)
✔ Omit this activity. You can use it in Module Four if you wish.

Stewardship-based Budgets (p. 27)
✔ The handout "My Monthly Budget" (p. 147) lists an item called "Stewardship/Giving Back." This might be a low-key way to introduce the idea of giving to others and giving back to God. (Participants will use this worksheet throughout the program and make changes as new concepts are introduced; they can adjust their stewardship budget as this becomes a more meaningful practice to them.)

HELP LINE

Market Economics. While it is valuable for participants to develop an understanding of the larger economic system (Module One/Session 1) that impacts their lives, some may find this information difficult to understand or to apply to their immediate situation. If you don't already know your group, you'll want to get to know as much as you can about each participant during the first two sessions (Module 1) before considering the changes for Module 2 we've suggested on page 17.

Module Two/Session 1: Market Economics (pp. 42-50)

✔ If the majority of participants in your group are at the very basic stages of money management—concerned with making ends meet, learning to balance a checkbook, and so on—you might decide to omit this session. You could spend the time instead focusing on tracking expenses (see Option 1. Keeping Financial Records, Module One/Session 1, p. 28), budgeting (see Stewardship-based Budgets, Module One/Session 1, p. 27), opening a checking or savings account (see Option 1. Checking and Savings Accounts, Module Three/Session 2, p. 84), balancing a checkbook, and so on. Working one-on-one in mentor/participant teams may be the most effective way to teach these skills.

Module Two/Session 2: Materialism vs. Values (pp. 51-61)

✔ It's almost impossible to talk about materialism without talking about values. By this time in your schedule, participants may be getting a sense that Christian values taught in God's Word can redirect our thinking and actions. We suggest that you present this session as outlined in the guide, being careful not to put down those who do not share your own values. Acknowledge that we all struggle with the influences of our materialistic culture.

HELP LINE

Investing. The session on investing (Module Three/Session 5) can be very intimidating to a participant who is struggling to make ends meet. If most of your group is just beginning to save for the future or consider buying a home, perhaps they are not ready for much more information at this point. Consider the changes for this session we've suggested below and on page 18.

Module Three/Session 5: Investing (pp. 105-116)

Savings vs. Investments (p. 109)

✔ We suggest that you use this first activity to introduce participants to the next level of financial security (see transparency master "Changing Behavior—Stepping Toward Financial Security," p. 134), following the sequence of Module Three.

Investing for Retirement (p. 110)

✔ If no one in your group has held a job in the past or if no one is presently working, you may want to omit this activity. However, it's likely that some or all of those in your group will have some work history and prior or present investment in the Social Security (U.S.) or Old Age Security (Canada) program. Use this activity to help them see the importance of starting now to plan for retirement. Then if some seem ready to go further, continue with the rest of the activities outlined in the guide (pp. 111-114). Those not interested could probably benefit more from spending extra time with their mentors on topics covered in previous sessions.

Investment Options (p. 111) and Return vs. Risk (p. 112)

✔ You may want to use a small group presentation along with one-on-one mentoring to present more detailed information about investing only to those who are ready for this information.

Faith-based Investing (p. 113)

✔ This is another activity applying Christian values to financial decisions.

Be especially sensitive to participants who may not be at this stage in their faith-based financial journey. Consider how or if you will present this activity so as not to offend them.

Module One

Setting the Course

Session 1: Stewardship

Session 2: Money and Me

Setting the Course

Session 1: Stewardship

Session Focus

We are all God's stewards and will be held accountable for how we use the gifts God has given us.

Session Goals

Participants will

- realize how the *Faith and Finances* program can help them learn to manage their money.
- learn what the Bible says about being a steward.
- define an economically healthy community.
- develop a stewardship-based budget.

Session Brief

ACTIVITIES	MINUTES	MATERIALS
Building Community Welcome Discussion Prayer	10-15	Beverage and snack, nametags, pens, pencils

Getting Started
Program Introduction
	10-15	Transparencies or photocopies:
		    "Biblical Guidelines for Stewardship" (p. 129)
		    "*Faith and Finances*: A Brief Overview" (p. 130)
		Overhead projector

Spiritual Reflection	10	Bibles (one for each participant), markers (optional)

Application Activities
A Steward Is . . .
Mind Map
Budgets
	
	10
	15-20
	25-40
		
		Chalkboard/chalk or newsprint/marker
		
		Handful of coins from pocket or billfold, calculators
		    (optional), pocket-type folders (one for each participant)
		Handouts (one photocopy for each participant):
		    "Where Is My Money Going?" (p. 146)
		    "My Monthly Budget" (p. 147)

Follow-up Activity	5	Notebook, two-column ledger, envelopes (see Option 1, p. 28)
Wrap-up	5	

For the Leader

The Christian faith community is divided between two gospel interpretations regarding wealth. Based on an assumption that consumption equals happiness, one side emphasizes that with faith comes a promise of financial success and a comfortable lifestyle. Christian societal critic Orlando Costas describes this view as creating a "conscience-soothing Jesus . . . , a pocket God . . . , and an escapist church" (*Christ Outside the Gate*, Orbis Books, 1982, p. 80).

This interpretation ignores these words from Scripture:

> *Now listen, you who say, "Today or tomorrow we will go to this or that city, spend a year there, carry on business and make money." Why, you do not even know what will happen tomorrow. What is your life? You are a mist that appears for little while and then vanishes. Instead, you ought to say, "If it is the Lord's will, we will live and do this or that." As it is, you boast and brag. All such boasting is evil.*
>
> —James 4:13-16

The second interpretation promotes a lifestyle of stewardship. For those of us who have grown up in the North American consumer society, this can be a difficult and demanding choice. We are only dimly aware that we are slaves to our money; we feel free because we are able to purchase what we want and need. However, like any other addict, we think the solution to our craving is one more fix; whether rich or poor, we buy more things to feel better.

Only through the power of the Holy Spirit can we break free of our consumer addiction and seek a better way. Three biblical principles will guide us toward faith-based stewardship:

- We must recognize that all of life is a gift from God.
  Our consumer culture falsely says, "We deserve this; life owes us." God has created this world and given us the responsibility to care for it, to practice stewardship.

- We must confess that our sins damage and even destroy some of this gift.
  The creation can be misused in a thousand different ways—from wasting of resources to unjust distribution of the earth's resources. The fraction of the world's people who live in communities of wealth practice a vicious cycle of work more/consume more, while the world's disadvantaged communities feel a sense of being on the outside, looking in on the economic action.

- We must realize that the world is not *mine* but *ours*.
  We must embrace stewardship as an alternative to materialism, to consumerism, to possessive individualism. This alternative requires refocusing both on our own decisions and actions and on our community, where we move from a *me* logic to a *we* logic. God calls us to make this world a home for everyone.

HELP LINE

We've suggested that you share these three principles with the participants as part of the introduction to the program (see Getting Started, p. 22). We've included a transparency master of this information in the reproducible materials section of this guide (see "Biblical Guidelines for Stewardship," p. 129).

If we live committed to stewardship, we will be free from a consumerist mentality. We will see ourselves called to a cause: to manage ourselves and our resources in service to God, our families, our neighbors, and ourselves. We will realize that all we possess is to be used to serve God, and for that we say, "Thank you, Jesus."

Building Community

10-15 minutes

1. It's important to spend time in each session building community. During this first session you will want to make sure everyone feels welcomed and leaves with a sense of what the program is all about. If you already have mentors assigned to work one-on-one, you'll want to introduce participants to their individual mentors right away.

2. We suggest you offer a beverage and snack as people arrive and have nametags, pens, and pencils available for leaders and participants. Allow a few minutes for informal visiting before you begin the session.

3. Then invite everyone to your discussion area. (Make sure the room is set up to encourage discussion and so that everyone can see any visuals you'll be using.) Ask participants and leaders to think about the best gift they've ever received from someone.

   With the entire group or in mentor/participant teams, have them share answers to these questions:

   ■ **What gift did you receive?**
   ■ **What was the occasion?**
   ■ **Why was the gift so memorable or meaningful?**

4. Offer a brief prayer thanking God for all good gifts and for each person present.

Getting Started

10-15 minutes

HELP LINE

Spend the next part of the session setting the stage for the program. If you are using this program as a side-door ministry to people in your community who are not members of your church or any Christian church, the concept of steward-ship may be very unfamiliar—even threatening—to them. If this is your situation, we suggest that you omit the first step below and save this activity for Module Four (see also Alternative Program Plans, p. 16).

1. Invite group members to think about the word *gift* from God's point of view. God has given us everything—and God has asked us to be *stewards* (care-takers) of the gifts we have received. Explain that the Bible has a lot to say about how we use God's gifts. Share the three principles summarized on the transparency (or handout) "Biblical Guidelines for Stewardship (p. 129). Ask participants these questions:

   ■ **How does our world of consumerism try to lead us away from these bib-lical guidelines?**

■ **What thoughts and actions might show that we're more in tune with our North American consumer society than with God's Word?**

2. Affirm group members for wanting to change and promise that they will be helped on their journey through this program. Use the transparency (or handout) *"Faith and Finances: A Brief Overview"* (p. 130) to introduce the four modules and session topics. Give everyone an opportunity to ask questions about the program, the schedule, what's expected of participants, the role of leaders, and so on.

Spiritual Reflection

10 minutes

HELP LINE

In this first session, we're introducing you to a suggested format for presenting the biblical perspective on stewardship. We recommend that you introduce the Scripture passage, inviting group members to follow along in the Bibles you've provided. (Depending on your group, you may want to mark the passage in each Bible. If you are working with adults who have difficulty reading, consider using an easier-to-read version—see "Language as Ministry" on p. 180 in the Appendix for suggested versions.)

Read the passage in sections, pausing after each section for a few moments of reflection. (You could read the passage to the group, or if group members are comfortable doing so, have them volunteer to read aloud.) We've provided some guidelines for reflection, but we encourage you to add your own insights and to be open to response from participants as well.

Depending on how you've organized your program, you may wish to have mentors present this part of the session as a one-on-one reflection time. Be sensitive to the fact that this may be the first time some in your group have ever used a Bible or heard God's Word applied to our everyday lives.

In Matthew 14, Jesus teaches us that stewardship requires compassion, a plan, and action. First we see Jesus' compassion (vv. 13-15).

> *When Jesus heard [of John the Baptist's death], he withdrew by boat privately to a solitary place. Hearing of this, the crowds followed him on foot from the towns. When Jesus landed and saw a large crowd, he had compassion on them and healed their sick. As evening approached, the disciples came to him and said, "This is a remote place, and it's already getting late. Send the crowds away, so they can go to the villages and buy themselves some food."*

It was late in the day at a remote location with no visible food supply. The disciples were eager to send the crowd away before hunger became a burden for the crowd and for themselves. To imagine how the disciples felt, picture the homeless pleading for money along Michigan Avenue in Chicago while harried workers, tourists, and shoppers try to discern what is their responsibility.

We can understand the disciples' response. Didn't they feel hungry and have nothing themselves? Was anyone looking out for them? They got stuck in their own lack of planning, wondering how could they be expected to help feed such a large group. However, Jesus, looking beyond himself and through his compassion for the people, had already devised a plan (vv. 16-19).

> Jesus replied, "They do not need to go away. You give them something to eat."
>
> "We have here only five loaves of bread and two fish," they answered.
>
> "Bring them here to me," he said. And he directed the people to sit down on the grass.

Finally Jesus put his stewardship plan into motion (vv. 19-21). He took action. And we learn that when the disciples acted, following Jesus' instruction, many more than 5,000 were fed.

> Taking the five loaves and the two fish and looking up to heaven, he gave thanks and broke the loaves. Then he gave them to the disciples, and the disciples gave them to the people. They all ate and were satisfied, and the disciples picked up twelve basketfuls of broken pieces that were left over. The number of those who ate was about five thousand men, besides women and children.

This story demonstrates that we learn compassion when our own inclinations and desires are brought face to face with the situation and needs of other people. We become stewards when we to listen for God's plan or God's command and, in response, take action, putting other people's needs ahead of our wants.

This compassion, in combination with biblical hope, offers peace for both rich and poor. Stewardship might be best expressed in these words:

> As stewards of a vineyard and keepers of the land,
> we wish to serve our Maker and follow his command
> to ever love our neighbor and justice to maintain.
> We search in new directions for justice and for peace;
> rejoicing in our labors, God's blessings will not cease.
> We wish to heal what's broken; we seek to ease the pain.

> —Text: Frank De Vries, "As Stewards of a Vineyard," © 1970, Christian Labour Association of Canada. Used by permission.

Notepad

Rev. John Timmer, a retired pastor in the Christian Reformed Church, has written about his parents' willingness to risk their lives to protect Jews in Europe during World War II. As a child he observed them hiding people in their home. He often asked, "Why did my parents do it? Why did they risk their own lives and possibly those of their six children? What madness possessed them to take such risks? The only reason I remember my father giving was this: 'As God shows compassion to us, so we must show compassion to others.'"

—John Timmer, "Half a Century Ago," *The Banner*, May 7, 1990, pp. 10-11. Used by permission.

Application Activities

A Steward Is . . .
10 minutes

1. Write the word *STEWARD* on the chalkboard or on newsprint. Record group members' responses to this question:

   ■ **What is a steward?**

   Possible responses might be caretaker, servant, follower, leader, manager. In all of these positions, we are responsible for maintaining what has been entrusted to us. We are stewards of everything God has given to us.

2. Part of being a steward is giving to others from what God has given us. Write the word *GIVING* on the chalkboard or newsprint. Record responses to this question:

   ■ **What can we give to others as stewards of what God has given to us?**

   Help the group to understand that giving can mean giving money to a church in the form of tithes and offerings, donating money or food and other tangible items to charity, volunteering time and talents, offering encouragement and prayers, and so on. In so doing, we give thanks to God and worship and praise God.

3. If you have time, ask the group to imagine that they have a million dollars that they've decided to keep for themselves . . . and then to imagine that they have a thousand dollars that they want to share with others . . . or only a bowl of soup to offer a friend. Encourage them to imagine how "rich" their lives would be in each of these situations. Emphasize that it isn't how much or how little we have that keeps us from being good stewards; it's how we take care of what God has given us that matters. Each one of us can be a part of making God's world a home for everyone.

Mind Map: A Healthy Economic Community
15-20 minutes

1. Use mind mapping to help participants visualize what it means to live in community. Write the word *COMMUNITY* inside a circle in the middle of the chalkboard or newsprint. (Make the circle large enough to add two more words later.) Ask participants to brainstorm what businesses, organizations, and other resources make up their community and help them in their day-to-day living. Write each of the suggestions in smaller circles surrounding the central circle. Responses might include schools, churches, banks, stores, parks, Social Services, and so on. Some of the suggestions may flow from words or phrases suggested previously; if so, connect them. Some might be closely associated; try to place them in close proximity. If a suggestion seems

to duplicate a previous one, ask the person who suggested it and the group to determine if it is repetitive.

HELP LINE

Your mind map might start out looking something like this:

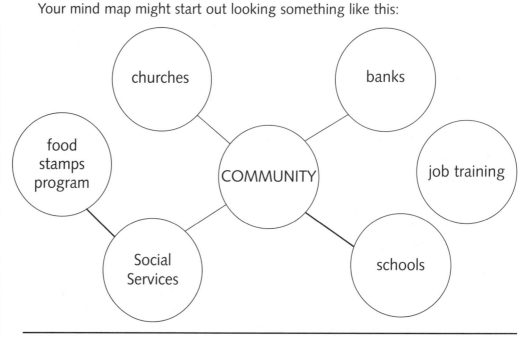

2. Introduce the concept of *healthy community* and insert the word *HEALTHY* into the center circle. Ask the group to add words that describe healthy communities. Responses might include clean parks, safe schools, safe neighborhoods, high moral values, acceptance of others, and so on. Write these responses in new circles and connect them to related words already on the mind map.

3. Then add the word *ECONOMIC* to the center circle, and ask participants to describe what makes a healthy economic community. Responses might include good paying jobs, on-the-job training, adequate child care, fair banking practices, equal access (non-discrimination) to jobs and resources, public transportation, and so on. Some of these ideas may have already been suggested, but add any that aren't already on the mind map, connecting them to related circles as appropriate.

4. If you have time, discuss some or all of the following questions.

■ **Why is it important to live in a healthy economic community?**

You might suggest that just as "it takes a village to raise a child," it takes an entire community to raise individuals and families who are economically healthy. If one suffers, we all suffer.

■ **How can the economic health of your community affect your personal assets?**

Note that property values decrease in areas of distressed community and high crime. Healthy communities can actually build wealth.

■ **How can you help make your community a healthy one?**

You or others in the group might suggest getting involved in block clubs, community policing, and so on.

■ **How can one's faith contribute to an economically healthy individual or family?**

Science now tells us that faith leads to good health, just as our genes increase the likelihood of good physical health. This appears to take place through a change of habits and character, and transformed habits and character lead to good financial health.

Stewardship-based Budgets
25-40 minutes

This faith-based program will help participants manage their money so that they can become part of economically healthy communities. The first step is to look honestly at one's own economic health, recognizing areas that need a "dose" of new knowledge and changed behaviors.

1. Empty a handful of coins out of your pocket or billfold onto the table in front of your group. Wonder how you'll spend this money during the next few days and ask for suggestions from the group. Admit that you might not have a very good idea of where this money went by the end of the week.

2. Distribute photocopies of the handout "Where Is My Money Going?" (p. 146). Read the directions to the participants, and allow time for them to complete the worksheet. (You may want to have calculators handy.) Establish accountability for each member's plan to save by cutting out unnecessary purchases for one month. Emphasize that even saving one dollar a week is progress, because it's the changed behavior that's important. By developing the habit of saving regularly, one dollar a week could become twenty dollars a week.

HELP LINE

To encourage accountability, you can allow time during the next four sessions for a "save-in" like the Weight Watchers weigh-in, or you might prefer to have mentors follow up on this commitment to save. Talk about how difficult it is to change old habits, and celebrate the progress made each week.

3. Distribute photocopies of the handout "My Monthly Budget" (p. 147). Have participants complete as much of this worksheet during the session as possible, and ask them to bring the completed worksheet to the next session. Again, you may want to provide calculators. Point out that the first expense item is for stewardship or giving back. This is shifting our thinking from *mine* to *ours*—it's a step of faith.

Notepad

You will come across advice in various money management resources that suggests budgeting for expenses something like this:

- Food 20%
- Health care 5%
- Clothing 5%
- Transportation 20%
- Personal and miscellaneous items 10%
- Insurance and emergencies 5%
- Retirement savings 5%
- Housing 30%

—Karen Chan and others, *All My Money*, 1997, University of Illinois Cooperative Extension Service.

We suggest you use these percentages only as a guideline when working with participants. Notice that nothing is budgeted for *giving back* to God or to others. Although each participant's situation is different, you can encourage each one to put stewardship first by avoiding unnecessary expenses and by cutting back on other expenses.

Some participants may need to look up income and expense information at home. If so, have them bring the completed budget worksheet back to the next session. (Provide inexpensive pocket-type folders for each person to collect handouts you'll be using throughout the program.) Be sure to allow time to follow up on this exercise during your next session.

Follow-up Activity
5 minutes

Encourage participants to keep careful record of their income and expenses during the next month. If needed, mentors can demonstrate a simple record-keeping system in a one-on-one situation (see Option 1. Keeping Financial Records, below). Suggest that they write down expenses in a notebook (or ledger if they prefer) or keep bills, receipts, and so on in envelopes (one enve-lope for income records and one for each expense category). Remind partici-pants that you'll repeat the budgeting exercise at the end of the month to help them see how well they've stayed within their budget.

Wrap-up
5 minutes

If you used the transparency "Biblical Guidelines for Stewardship" (p. 129) earlier in the session (see Getting Started, p. 22), spend a few minutes review-ing the three biblical principles of faith-based stewardship. Clarify procedures for the next session (time, place, things to bring, and so on), and allow time for questions. Close with a brief prayer or time of praise.

Optional Activity

Use optional activities to extend the session or to meet specific needs of those in your group.

Option 1. Keeping Financial Records
Budgeting can be a difficult assignment if a person has no clear idea of income and expenditures. If you find that's true for some of your participants, you'll want to help them set up a simple system for keeping records. For your first session, we suggest that you display a few supplies needed and a sample of these options: a notebook record, a two-column ledger, or an envelope sys-tem. Show a record of one month's income and expenses using each of these systems. (Use a budget that is representative of the lifestyle of the majority of your group.) Then schedule a time to work one-on-one with those who need to set up their own system, allowing them to choose the system that looks work-able for them.

Module One
Setting the Course

Session 2: Money and Me

Session Focus
Because we are God's stewards, it is our responsibility to learn to manage our money wisely.

Session Goals
Participants will

- learn what the Bible says about money.
- describe how past generations and people today put into practice what the Bible says about managing money.
- realize that they can learn new skills to manage their money.
- set financial goals in keeping with biblical principles.

Session Brief

ACTIVITIES	MINUTES	MATERIALS
Building Community	10-15	
Welcome		Refreshments, nametags, pens, pencils
Discussion		
Prayer		
Spiritual Reflection	15-20	Index cards (nine), Bibles (one for each person or small group), newsprint, markers
Application Activities		
Learning from Past Generations	10	Chalkboard/chalk or newsprint/marker
Learning from People Today	10-15	Newsprint and markers (for each small group)
"Save-in" or Mentoring	5-10	Handout: "Where Is My Money Going?" (from Session 1)
Personal Financial Audit	15-25	Calculators (optional) Handouts: "My Financial Picture" (p. 150, one photocopy for each participant) "My Monthly Budget" (from Session 1)
Setting Financial Goals	15-25	Handout (one photocopy for each participant): "My Financial Goals" (p. 151) Display of money management resources (see p. 36)
Follow-up Activity	5	
Wrap-up	5	

For the Leader

Faith-based stewardship calls us to manage our money in service to God, to our family, to our neighbors, and for our own well-being. But that is not the goal toward which our North American society pressures us. Our culture increasingly acts as if nothing should come between us and our money; we should believe that money talks and that the more we have, the better.

Amidst the clamor of commercials, billboards, and junk mail, we need to hear the voice of God calling us to set ourselves apart. John Ortberg, in his book *The Life You've Always Wanted* (Zondervan Publishing House, 1997, p. 90), writes:

> We live in a lethal environment. American society is filled with ideas and values and pressures and temptations about success and security and comfort and happiness that we will not even notice unless we withdraw on occasion. . . . The early church fathers placed such a premium on solitude because they considered society to be a shipwreck from which any sane person must swim for life. These people believed that to let oneself drift along, passively accepting the tenets and values of what they knew as society, was purely and simply a disaster. The apostle Paul put it this way: "Don't let the world around you squeeze you into its own mold."

Instead of listening for God's direction, we spend much of our time worrying about where our money is coming from and where it's going. Lloyd J. Ogilvie, in his book *Making Stress Work for You* (Word Books, 1984, pp. 148-151), contends that "dealing with money brings stress to poor and wealthy, to Christians and non-Christians alike." To help Christians manage their money in a way that "reflects our trust in God and our obedience to his will," Ogilvie offers these general principles (bulleted and italized below, with our comments added):

- *Base your financial dealings on the knowledge that all we are and have belongs to the Lord.*

Who we are and what we earn are not *our* gifts to God—they are *God's* gifts to us. Let go of the stress of self-effort and enjoy the gifts God has given you!

- *Ask God for a radical "to the roots" commitment of all you have and are.*
  This will help you break free of our culture's expectations. This means surrendering the control center of your whole life—finances and all—to God.

- *Ask God's guidance in how to spend, earn, save, and give.*
  You'll be surprised at God's willingness to be involved in this area of your life!

- *Give the tithe (one-tenth) that belongs to God.*
  And then learn how to give more than that amount with freedom and joy.

Practice faith-promise giving! Yield your checkbook to become a channel for the unexpected income God can give you for special kingdom causes.

As a leader, modeling and teaching God-controlled money management is your challenge. Consider these words of Paul, his charge to Timothy, your calling:

> Tell those who are rich [or poor] in this world not to be proud [or discouraged] and not to trust in their money, which will soon be gone. But their trust should be in the living God, who richly gives us all we need for our enjoyment. Tell [everyone] to use their money to do good [to serve God, their family, their neighbors, and for their own well-being]. They should be rich in good works and should give generously to those in need, always being ready to share with others whatever God has given them. By doing this they will be storing up their treasure as a good foundation for the future so that they may take hold of real life.
>
> —1 Timothy 6:17-19, NLT

Building Community
10-15 minutes

1. If you've already assigned mentors to work one-on-one, make sure they're on hand to greet their participants. Offer refreshments as people arrive and have nametags, pens, and pencils available for leaders and participants. Allow a few minutes for informal visiting before you begin the session.

2. Then invite everyone to your discussion area. Ask mentors and participants, working in pairs, to think about this old adage attributed to Ben Franklin: "A penny saved is a penny earned." Have them recall a time when they saved little by little and finally were able to buy something they really needed or were able to give a special gift to someone else. Have them share answers to these questions with the entire group:

   ■ **Where did the money come from?**
   ■ **Where was the money kept?**
   ■ **For whom and for what was the money spent?**
   ■ **Why do you remember this experience?**

   The stories you hear might be precious childhood memories or bright spots in tough times. Recognize God's goodness in these stories, and offer a brief prayer of thanks for God's gifts and for each person present.

Spirtual Reflection
15-20 minutes

1. The Bible calls us to be stewards of everything God has given us. But does God's Word give us directions about managing our money? Invite the group to read and discuss several passages to see exactly what God says about our money.

   Provide each individual (or small group) with Bibles (with selected passages marked with an index card), a sheet of newsprint, and a marker. Have them read the assigned passage and write down what they think the verse is telling them about money. Tape the responses to the wall for group discussion. (Suggested responses are given with each Scripture passage on pp. 32-33, but be open to other conclusions group members offer.)

HELP LINE

Ahead of time, write the location of each Scripture passage on separate index cards. Use the cards to mark the specific passages in the Bibles group members will use. Depending on the size of your group, assign an individual or a small group to each passage. (If your group is small, assign more than one passage to each person or omit some of the verses. Or if you prefer, read and discuss all the passages together with the entire group, or pair mentors with participants.)

Dishonest money dwindles away, but he who gathers money little by little makes it grow.

—Proverbs 13:11

—Get money honestly; save and spend wisely.

■

A good man is more desirable than great riches; to be esteemed is better than silver or gold.

—Proverbs 22:1

—A person's character is more precious than money.

■

She [a woman of noble character] watches over the affairs of her household and does not eat the bread of idleness.

—Proverbs 31:27

—One who works and manages his or her money will be respected.

■

Whoever loves money never has money enough; whoever loves wealth is never satisfied with his income.

—Ecclesiastes 5:10

—A person who loves money becomes greedy and unhappy.

■

"Bring the whole tithe into the storehouse, that there may be food in my house. Test me in this," says the LORD Almighty, "and see if I will not throw open the floodgates of heaven and pour out so much blessing that you will not have room enough for it."

—Malachi 3:10

—When we give back to God, God will bless us abundantly.

■

[Jesus, teaching the crowd on the mountainside, said,] "No one can serve two masters. Either he will hate the one and love the other, or he will be devoted to the one and despise the other. You cannot serve both God and Money."

—Matthew 6:24

—Serve God, not money. God will take care of our needs.

■

John [the Baptist] answered [the crowd who had come to be baptized], "The man with two tunics should share with him who has none, and the one who has food should do the same."

—Luke 3:11

—Share whatever God has given you with those in need.

■

*He [John the Baptist] replied [to the tax collectors who came to be
baptized], "Don't extort money and don't accuse people falsely—be
content with your pay."*

—Luke 3:14

—Be honest; be satisfied with what God provides.

■

*Now about the collection for God's people. . . . On the first day of
every week, each one of you should set aside a sum of money in
keeping with his income. . . .*

—1 Corinthians 16:1, 2

—Make giving to God's work a regular habit regardless of how little or
how much you have.

■

*But godliness with contentment is great gain. For we brought nothing
into the world, and we can take nothing out of it. But if we have
food and clothing, we will be content with that. People who want to
get rich fall into temptation and a trap and into many foolish and
harmful desires that plunge men into ruin and destruction. For the
love of money is a root of all kinds of evil. Some people, eager for
money, have wandered from the faith and pierced themselves with
many griefs.*

—1 Timothy 6:6-10

—Loving money can get us into all kinds of trouble; trusting and serving
God will bring contentment.

2. Conclude your reflection on these Scripture passages by reading this final
verse to the group:

*For everything that was written in the past was written to teach us,
so that through endurance and the encouragement of the Scriptures
we might have hope.*

—Romans 15:4

Application Activities

Learning from Past Generations
15 minutes

1. Most of us would agree that people who lived in the first half of the last century were more thrifty or frugal than we are today. Ask the group to think about their own ancestors as they reflect on the questions below. (Record responses on chalkboard or newsprint.)

   ■ What did the "pioneers" in your family do to increase income?
   ■ How did they reduce their living expenses?
   ■ How did these money management practices create a more positive future for their families?
   ■ What advice from God's Word were these people following?
   ■ What can we learn from these people?

   In response to the last question, group participants may suggest staying in school, getting on-the-job training, and so on as ways to eventually increase income. For decreasing expenses, they might suggest carpooling, swapping day care, stopping gambling, spending less on fast foods, and paying bills on time. The group might also suggest being dependable at work, caring for their children, and planning ahead as ways to improve their future. These are all part of being good stewards of what God has given us.

HELP LINE

It may be that participants in this program cannot think of anyone in their families who modeled good money management. In that case, they have identified a major missing piece in their life experience that probably has hampered them from becoming good money managers. For these people, the mentor's role will be especially important as the mentor encourages them to break the cycle of poverty their families may have experienced for generations. Be sensitive also to those who are hearing about biblically based stewardship for the first time.

Learning from People Today
15-20 minutes

As we look around our communities, we can find examples of good things people do with their money. Sometimes these people are wealthy; sometimes people who have very little work together to provide something good for others.

1. Depending on the size of your group, divide into groups of 3-4. Give each group a sheet of newsprint and a marker. Have each group make a list of good things people in your community have done with their money that

have benefited others. Then have members suggest which one or two items on the list rank at the top.

2. Have each group present their list and explain why they ranked the one or two items at the top. Have the entire group select from these top-ranked items the one they think most closely follows what the Bible says about money.

3. Look back over the lists and have group members reflect on these questions:

   ■ **Which of these giving acts would you have liked to be a part of?**
   ■ **What might have prevented you from giving to this cause?**

   Perhaps many in your group are unable to give at this point in their lives. Conclude that when we learn to manage our money in a stewardly, biblical way, we will be able to give back to God and others. Affirm participants for taking the first steps on this faith journey.

HELP LINE

This might be a good time to follow up on the worksheet "Where Is My Money Going?" introduced in the first session (see p. 27 and the handout on p. 146). Conduct a "save-in" or have mentors work with their participants to discuss problems and celebrate progress.

Personal Financial Audit
20 minutes

Last session participants were asked to complete the worksheet "My Monthly Budget." The following activity will use information from that worksheet to help participants conduct a personal financial audit (a picture of their current financial situation).

HELP LINE

We suggest that mentors work one on one with participants to complete the personal financial audit exercise. This will give the mentor as well as the participant a picture of income in relation to expenses and assets available to meet short-term and long-term goals. It's an important process to complete before setting new financial goals.

1. To encourage participants to open up, ask each mentor/participant team to share with each other one little known financial fact about themselves. Share a fact about yourself to get them started. (For example, maybe you save your loose change in a gallon jar that you lug to the bank to have counted—and then quickly spend it on something just for yourself. Or perhaps you lived on a diet of beans and bread while working your way through school. Maybe you've experienced financial hardship because of a poor investment.)

Since this exercise may reveal very personal facts, use your best judgment to determine if you want participants to share beyond their team. Help the group to recognize that financial issues face us all throughout our lifetime and that the more we know about our financial picture, the better we can solve these problems.

Notepad

When Abraham Lincoln was asked about a neighbor's financial picture, he replied: "He has a wife and baby; together, they ought to be worth $50,000 to any man. Secondly, he has an office with a table worth $1.50 and three chairs worth $1."

—Clifton Fadiman, editor, *The Little, Brown Book of Anecdotes*, Little, Brown and Company, 1985.

2. Distribute photocopies of the handout "My Financial Picture" (p. 150). Provide calculators if your group used them last time. Have participants complete this worksheet using information from their worksheet "My Monthly Budget" (from Session 1, p. 147).

3. Ask participants if they would like to change their financial picture. In teams or as a whole group discuss these questions:

- What financial challenges are you facing?
- What assets would you like to acquire?
- What skills do you need in order to improve your financial picture?

Setting Financial Goals
15-25 minutes

Doing nothing about our current financial situation can destroy our lives, but learning new skills to manage our money can help us reach our goals.

1. Distribute photocopies of the handout "My Financial Goals" (p. 151). Invite participants to work through the process with their mentors to set short-term and long-term financial goals that reflect the biblical principles you've discussed.

2. If time permits, ask the mentor/participant teams to identify ways and places where individuals and families can find information about managing their money that will help them reach the short-term and long-term goals they've set.

HELP LINE

Arrange a display of resources from various places that participants can use to help them achieve their goals. Include books from libraries and bookstores, fliers about seminars offered in the area, government publications (check with your local Cooperative Extension Service), magazines, Internet printouts, and so on. Encourage group members to bring to future sessions other resources they've found helpful, and spend a few minutes each time you meet reviewing the resources that are available. (You could even set up a check-out system if you wish so that participants can take the resources home for closer examination.)

Follow-up Activity

5 minutes

Encourage participants to take one step toward meeting one of their long-term goals. Perhaps they need information about buying a car or home or need to know if they qualify for a certain government-sponsored program. Suggest they find written information or make an appointment with a banker or others "in the know." Invite them to report back to the group what they've learned about meeting a specific goal (use this as your community building exercise next session).

Wrap-up

5 minutes

Reemphasize the focus of Module One: faith-based stewardship calls us to manage our money in service to God, to our family, to our neighbors, and for our own well-being.

Review procedures for the next session, and remind participants to bring their folders with completed worksheets to each session. Close with a brief prayer or time of praise.

Optional Activities

Use these optional activities to extend the session or to meet specific needs of those in your group. Each of the options suggested below may be worthy of a separate session depending on the needs of participants.

Option 1. The Tax Bite

Most of us were—and probably still are—shocked at the amount of money taken out of our first paycheck for taxes. In the U.S., wages are subject to federal income, Social Security, and Medicare taxes, and wage earners may also need to pay state and city income taxes. Consumers, regardless if they are wage earners, may also pay property taxes on real estate and sales taxes on certain goods and services.

In Canada, wages are subject to federal and provincial income tax, Social Insurance taxes, and deductions for the Canada Pension Plan. Canadians also pay real estate taxes, goods and services taxes and provincial sales tax, and taxes on gasoline, alcohol, and cigarettes.

1. Using a calculator and writing your calculations on the chalkboard or newsprint, calculate wages for a forty-hour week at the minimum wage paid in your community. Multiply this figure by 50 weeks to calculate the annual before-tax income. Use a Federal tax guide and a state or province tax guide to determine the income tax owed on this income; subtract this amount from the annual income. Subtract other payroll taxes (Social Security and Medicare in the U.S. or Old Age Security in Canada).

Notepad

Corporations as well as individuals are taxed, but in the U.S. the burden has been shifting from corporations to individuals. According to the Bureau of the Census, Government Finances Division, corporations paid $.76 for every dollar paid by an individual in 1950-54, $.41 for every dollar in 1965-69, and $.21 for every dollar in 1985-92.

Most Canadians pay less in income taxes than U.S. citizens with equivalent incomes. This is due largely to the fact that Canada practices *progressive* taxation, taxing the wealthy at higher rates than those with low and moderate incomes. In the U.S., the very rich raise the income average but are taxed less than their counterparts in Canada.

—Michel Wolfson and Brian Murphy, "Struggle to Pay Rent," *The Toronto Star*, November 6, 1999, p. A1.

2. Spend a few minutes discussing these questions about the tax system:

■ **Why do we pay taxes?**

Federal, state/province, and city taxes fund welfare programs, education, highways, and numerous other programs in both the U.S. and Canada.

■ **Would families be able to provide these programs without government taxation and management?**
■ **Whose responsibility is it to manage our tax dollars? Whose responsibility is it to manage what's left (our after-tax dollars)?**

As citizens, we expect our governments to manage our tax dollars wisely. We can have a voice in this process by voting and becoming involved in the decision-making process, especially at the local level. Emphasize that it's our after-tax income that we as individuals need to be most concerned about managing.

HELP LINE

For the budgeting process introduced in this session, we will ask participants to work with after-tax income since this is the portion of income over which they can exercise the most control. Later, as you discuss investments (Module Three/Session 5) you may talk about sheltering a portion of one's income from taxes, but for now that likely will not be a major concern of most participants.

3. If you have time, have each participant work with his or her mentor to estimate after-tax income from wages or business. This figure will be needed to complete the handout "My Monthly Budget."

Option 2. Building Assets

Introduce the group to an asset building strategy such as the Individual Development Account (IDA). This program is designed to promote asset accumulation among low-income and other disadvantaged groups in the United States. Similar in structure to U.S. Individual Retirement Accounts (IRAs) and Canadian Registered Retirement Savings Plans (RRSPs), money put into these IDA accounts can only be used for purchasing a first home, for education or job training expenses, or for starting a small business.

HELP LINE

Individual Development Accounts "are managed by community organizations, and accounts are held at local financial institutions. Contributions for lower-income participants are matched using both private and public sources. Additionally, all participants take an economic literacy class in which they work with a trained facilitator on the basics of money management, cleaning up their credit, and setting up a budgeting and savings schedule" ("What Are Individual Development Accounts?" Corporation for Enterprise Development).

MidAmerica Leadership Foundation has IDA partnerships with banks in Chicago. Participants must agree to make a minimum deposit of $25 per month for three years. The account can be maintained for a maximum of four years, although contributions will only be matched for three years. If the account is not used within a four-year time period (to purchase a first home, to start a small business, or for post-secondary education), the IDA account will be closed. The participant can transfer the IDA to another eligible family member or take out the savings (minus the matching funds).

For more information about IDAs, contact

Corporation for Enterprise Development, National Office
777 North Capitol NE, Suite 410
Washington D.C. 20002
Phone: 202-408-9788
Fax: 202-408-9793
E-mail: cfed@cfed.org

Option 3. Destroying Assets

As gambling has become socially acceptable, the voice of the church, which has traditionally condemned gambling as immoral and destructive, has been drowned out. But faith-based groups need to call gambling what it is: irresponsible behavior, leaving to chance what God wants us to be responsible for. Gambling seduces many people with false promises and solutions of easy winnings and gain without effort. It encourages coveting a lifestyle that may well be beyond our reach—and even immoral. Gambling, American style, has been cleaned up, civilized, licensed, government approved, and transformed into supposedly family-friendly entertainment. But is it? Ask your group to consider this question:

- **What good has gambling done for people in your community? in your church family? in your own family?**

HELP LINE

Recognize that gambling may be a very sensitive topic and one that might bring hurt, anger, guilt, and shame to the surface for individuals in your group. You may want to invite a Christian counselor who works with families in crisis because of gambling addiction to speak to your group. Mentors will want to be especially alert to signs of trouble and help participants connect to those who can help the healing begin.

Notepad

Gambling is an ancient vice that has soured lives and destroyed families for generations. By 1910, American reformers succeeded in banning nearly all gambling. But since 1978, gambling has made a breathtaking comeback. In 1999, Americans legally wagered more than $550 billion, which is more than three times the revenues of General Motors, the country's largest corporation.

—"Gambling with the Enemy," *Christianity Today*, May 18, 1998, p. 24.

Module Two
Building Knowledge

Session 1: Market Economics

Session 2: Materialism vs. Values

HELP LINE

While it is valuable for participants to develop an understanding of the larger economic system described in Module Two/Session 1, some may find this information difficult to understand or to apply to their immediate situation. If you don't already know your group, you'll want to get to know as much as you can about each participant during the first two sessions (Module One) before deciding to use Module Two. You may choose to omit Session 1 altogether or to use it later in the program—see also Alternate Program Plans (p. 17).

Module Focus
Our economic system impacts our lives and challenges our values.

Building Knowledge

Session 1: Market Economics

Session Focus

Learning basic economic principles can help us survive, even thrive, as children of God in a capitalistic system that requires a market economy.

Session Goals

Participants will

- define terms that describe our market economy.
- identify the benefits of a market economy.
- understand how our economic system affects their lives.
- understand how to participate in our market economy from a faith-based perspective.

Session Brief *

ACTIVITIES	MINUTES	MATERIALS
Building Community Welcome Sharing Resources Prayer	10-15	Refreshments
Spiritual Reflection	10	Bibles (one for each group member)
Application Activities Understanding Our Market Economy	15-20	Chalkboard/chalk or newsprint/marker Transparency or photocopies: "Our Market-based Economy . . . " (p. 131) Overhead projector
Vocabulary	10-20	Handout (one photocopy for each participant): "The Language of Our Market Economy" (p. 153) Pens/pencils
Market Simulation	20-30	Materials for buying and selling (see Help Line, p. 47)
Market Role Play	15-25	Transparency or photocopies: "The Market Process" (p. 132) Photocopy of "Market Process Role Play Cards" (p. 154) Gadget (see Help Line, p. 48)
Follow-up Activity	5	
Wrap-up	5	Transparency: "Our Market-based Economy . . . "

* See note on previous page and Alternate Program Plans (p. 17) before planning this session.

For the Leader

In primitive societies, people gathered and hunted for what they needed. But today, except in a few remote locations, individuals and families need to exchange money for goods and services. And just as an individual or a family needs money to meet basic needs and reach future goals, a society that wants to make progress beyond simple gathering must have an economic system in place that encourages people to produce more than is required for immediate needs.

Capitalism is organized around production. As a society becomes more complex and its members better educated, more specialized tasks and elaborate products emerge. Those with greater ability or opportunity are able to perform the more valued tasks and produce the more valued products. They then receive a larger share of the rising wealth of the society, creating disparity in wealth and power.

This drive for wealth and power may result in disregard for values such as loyalty and mutual commitment that once bound worker with owner and helpless dependents with other members of society in interdependency, respect, and trust. Such bonds have sometimes been replaced by expedient relationships that emphasize short-term gains and an attitude and ethic author Richard Sennett describes in a chilling one-liner: "If you don't take care of yourself, we'll do without you" (*The Corrosion of Character: The Personal Consequences of Work in the New Capitalism*, W. W. Norton Company, 1998, p. 142).

This is the very attitude Jesus warned against when addressing those who thought they could win God's favor simply by tithing:

> Woe to you teachers of the law and Pharisees, you hypocrites! You give a tenth of your spices. . . . But you have neglected the more important matters of the law—justice, mercy, and faithfulness. You should have practiced the latter, without neglecting the former.
>
> —Matthew 23:23

Christians face the challenge of practicing faith-based stewardship in a society that is increasingly polarized between the rich and the poor. Bill Shore, founder of the organization Share Our Strength, believes that opportunities based on person-to-person commitment will level the playing field. Quoting researcher and author Jonathan Freedman (*From Cradle to Grave: The Human Face of Poverty in America*), Shore advocates for programs that

> provide a way for two people—one in need of help and another wanting to help—to form a bond transforming *both their lives*. . . . It takes money, organization, and laws to maintain a social structure, but none of it works if there are not opportunities for people to meet and help each other along the way. . . . The most basic level of response is not governmental; it is intimate, one on one, neighbor to neighbor, family to family, community by community, hand by hand. . . .
>
> —Bill Shore, *Revolution of the Heart*, Riverhead Books, 1995, p. 8.

Building Community
10-15 minutes

---

1. Begin with a few minutes of informal visiting over refreshments.

2. As a follow-up activity to the previous session, participants were encouraged to find information they needed to reach their long-term goals. Invite group members to your discussion area to share their goal and a brief summary of the information they've collected.

3. Most likely, more than one person will benefit from the information shared. Express your appreciation for the sense of community developing within your group, and offer a brief prayer of thanks for each person and for the opportunity to help each other.

Spiritual Reflection
10 minutes

As we noted in Module One, God's Word has much to say about stewardship and money. Paul provides pastoral advice about gaining wealth in these words to Timothy (invite group members to follow along in their Bibles):

> *Command those who are rich in this present world not to be arrogant nor to put their hope in wealth, which is so uncertain, but to put their hope in God, who richly provides us with everything for our enjoyment. Command them to do good, to be rich in good deeds, and to be generous and willing to share. In this way they will lay up treasure for themselves as a firm foundation for the coming age, so that they may take hold of the life that is truly life.*

> —1 Timothy 6:17-19

We could quickly assume that Paul's words apply only to rich Christians, those who have accumulated more than they need in terms of earthly goods and who can afford to buy the services of others to make their lives easier. But Paul is stressing more the *uncertainty* of these riches than the amount. Each of us, regardless of how much or how little we own, must trust in God, who gives us everything we need.

Paul says that what God has given us is to be *enjoyed*. That seems almost too easy in our pleasure-seeking society, especially for those who have unlimited resources. But Paul very quickly presents a more difficult challenge: *do good, be generous, share!* Each of us can be rich in good deeds. When we share what God has so richly given us, we will experience genuine enjoyment and acquire a better and lasting wealth.

Application Activities

Understanding Our Market Economy
15-20 minutes

Even though some of the concepts of our market economy may seem irrelevant to those in your group struggling to make ends meet, they experience the workings of our market-based economy every day. It is our intention to give group members a basic understanding of our economic system so that they can participate more fully in the society around them.

1. Have group members empty the money out of their pockets or coin purses onto the table in front of them. Take a minute to have fun with this. Notice the "neat freaks" whose bills are crisp and straight and the "collectors" whose coins are mixed in with screws, toothpicks, gum, and the like. Then ask this question:

   ■ **How did you get this money?**

   Write the answers on a chalkboard or newsprint. Answers might include "I earned it at my job," "I sold Susie's bike," "I recycled pop cans," "Somebody liked my creative idea." Point out that some in the group got the money by providing *services* and others by selling *goods*.

2. Use the transparency (or handout) "Our Market-based Economy . . . " (p. 131) to introduce our economic system.

   Then brainstorm a list of words that are associated with market economics (free enterprise, profit, wealth, competition, private ownership of property, investing, choice, initiative, creativity, and so on.) Your group may also list words that describe a negative side of capitalism (greed, self-interest, power, and so on). Record responses on the transparency or have group members write the responses on their handouts.

3. Although there are negative sides to our market-based economy, in contrast to communism, it provides an opportunity for people to develop and maintain profitable businesses. Record responses on newsprint as your group brainstorms a list of positive contributions businesses make in a capitalistic society. Here are some possible contributions (some may have already been given in the previous step):

   ■ **production of new products and services.**
   Think of the array of products at a nearby supermarket or the list of services offered in the yellow pages of your local phone directory.

   ■ **market research to determine needs or discover better products.**
   Much research goes into the production of safe foods and drugs, for example, in our North American markets and results in products designed to increase our health and well-being.

Notepad

Our market-based economy depends on the exchange of goods and services for money. Will Durant (*The Story of Civilization I: Our Oriental Heritage*, Simon & Schuster, 1954, pp. 15-16) reports that in early times the means of exchange involved "dates, salt, skins, furs, ornaments, implements, and weapons. . . . Cattle were a convenient standard of value and medium of exchange among hunters and herders; they bore interest through breeding, and they transported themselves." Our word *capital*, Durant writes, goes back "through the French to the Latin 'capitale,' meaning property, and this in turn derives from 'caput,' meaning 'head'—i.e., of cattle. When metals were mined, they slowly replaced other articles as a standard of value . . . silver and gold became the money due to their little space and weight."

■ **hiring of unskilled and skilled workers.**

Consider what would happen to unemployment rates in your area if a large company moved into your community. What is the impact of on-the-job training, internships, and other such programs offered by many companies?

■ **paying higher wages.**

What effect would a profitable business in your community have in making wages more competitive? How often are earnings exchanged for goods and services in the community, thereby providing more goods and services?

■ **charitable contributions.**

Many businesses contribute to the public good by supporting local school fundraising campaigns, by offering scholarships, and by sponsoring or making major financial contributions to community service projects, buildings, and so on (Special Olympics, city museums, summer camps). Consider what benefits each of your group members have received because of these contributions.

Vocabulary

10-20 minutes

1. The language of our market-based economy is all around us. It's discussed in the newspaper, on TV, on the campaign trail, and in the coffee shop. To help group members zero in on some of these terms, distribute photocopies of the handout "The Language of Our Market Economy" (p. 153). Have participants match the words to the definitions.

2. Discuss the words and definitions, giving group members an opportunity to relate the terms to their own experience. For example, you might ask them to share what their favorite market is or a time when they noticed that their dollar bought less than it once did.

HELP LINE

Here's the answer key for the vocabulary match:

1. b. Market
2. c. Liability (debt)
3. e. Appreciates
4. g. Home
5. j. Income
6. i. Market-based economy
7. l. Net worth
8. f. Wealth
9. d. Depreciation
10. h. Car
11. k. Inflation
12. a. Assets

Market Simulation

20-30 minutes

1. Ahead of time, set up a situation that will introduce group members to the components and process of a market economy. The situation should generate competition, a desire to buy and sell, and an opportunity to profit from the market.

HELP LINE

There are many ways to conduct an activity that will introduce the components and process of a market. If you're working with a very small group or an individual, you could use play money and pictures of products from catalogs or store fliers. Talk about competitive prices, brand names, advertising, and so on. Or you might play a round of *Monopoly*, establishing new rules as needed to more quickly buy and sell property. (Watch property appreciate, and notice all the budgeting decisions made.)

If your group is larger, collect items from members of your church or community and set up a small garage sale. Use play or real money to buy, bargain, swap, and so on. Or try the following idea, which was successfully used while field-testing this program:

> *I bought a beanie baby ($6), a "grinch" ($6), and a small teddy bear ($4). I distributed the three objects to three of the participants, and gave three other participants $5 each. Group members were invited to buy or sell, and several transactions occurred that generated good discussion. For example, when one member made an offer and then withdrew it, we talked about how the market would handle a situation where someone reneged on a contract.*
>
> —Gary Nederveld, MidAmerica Leadership Foundation.

2. Allow time for discussion of questions like these:

   - **What happens to the price of a product if a less expensive but equally acceptable product (for example, generic drugs and foods) comes into the market?**
   - **What would happen if consumers boycotted a particular store because it sold pornographic material?**
   - **What happens to a company that produces a product that becomes a passing fad (Cabbage Patch dolls, Ford Thunderbirds, bell-bottoms, and so on)?**
   - **What gives a product (beanie babies, low-fat milk, 1955 Chevrolet, and so on) value?**

Market Role Play

15-25 minutes

1. The market-based economy is really a give-and-take process between investors, corporations (industry), businesses, and buyers (consumers). To illustrate this process, use the transparency (or handout) "The Market Process" (p. 132). Quickly point out the cyclic nature of the process without explaining it (leave the overhead on during the role play).

2. Ask for four volunteers (mentors can participate too) to play the parts of the investor, corporate CEO, retailer, and buyer. Provide photocopies of the "Market Process Role Play Cards" (p. 154), and ask the volunteers to follow the prompts and read the role play lines on the card.

HELP LINE

For the role play activity, purchase a gadget (apple corer, toddler's "sippy" cup with lid, pocket knife with "extras", and so on) that is useful, but not necessarily a "must have" item. Some of the role play will be ad-lib and will affect the profit or loss outcome (note the *ifs* in the summary statements below).

3. Using the transparency, summarize the process with these statements:

   ■ Investors put money in and get more money back *if* the corporation profits.
   ■ Corporations use the investor's money to produce goods (and services) and get more money back *if* businesses buy their product (or services).
   ■ Businesses make a profit *if* consumers buy this product.
   ■ Businesses will buy the product again *if* they make a profit, and corporations will continue to produce the product *if* sales remain strong.
   ■ Profitable corporations can do a lot of good. Profits guarantee the corporation a future in which they can grow, reward stockholders, produce new products, hire more people, and pay higher wages.

4. To help participants see how they can participate more fully in the market process, discuss these questions (record responses to the last three questions on the chalkboard or newsprint):

   ■ Who really "owns" the corporations?
   ■ Do you know anyone who is an "owner" of a corporation or a business?
   ■ What are the advantages to being an owner of a corporation or business?
   ■ What factors keep people from owning a business or investing in a corporation?
   ■ What does it take to be an investor?

Follow-up Activity
5 minutes

Encourage participants to share with three other people what they have learned about our market economy. Suggest that they revisit their monthly budget and short-term and long-term goals if they feel that investing should become part of their personal financial picture. Point out that you will talk more about this topic in Module Three, Session 5.

Wrap-up
5 minutes

Refer again to the transparency "Our Market-based Economy . . . " and emphasize that everyone plays a part in and is affected by our economic system. Review procedures for the next session, and remind participants to bring their folders with completed worksheets to each session. Close with a brief prayer or time of praise and thanksgiving for God's many blessings.

Optional Activities

Use these optional activities to extend the session or to meet specific needs of those in your group.

Option 1. Ripped Off?

If you are working with an inner-city group, present the following scenario:

Many people agree that capitalism can provide opportunities in low income areas, but it can also take advantage of people living in these neighborhoods. Anne S. Habiby of Competitive Inner City, a non-profit organization in Boston, says, "These are communities of large concentrated buying power with no competition. Our research indicates that there are a large number of inner-city retailers outperforming their suburban counterparts. We view the inner city as America's next great retail frontier."

—Christy Fisher, "City Lights Beckon to Business," *American Demographics*, October, 1997, pp. 45-46.

Discuss these questions:

- **Are these retailers providing a service to low income neighborhoods?**
- **Is this a great pocket of opportunity for everyone or a rip-off of the poor?**

Option 2. Discussion Starters

If you have time, consider some of these questions:

■ Does our market economy create conditions that lead to economic inequality in our community? If so, what must be done to protect the disadvantaged?

■ We know that the global economic system leads to wide disparities in wealth. Is this concentration of wealth an injustice?

■ How can the failure to advocate for more even distribution of wealth affect the future of families for several generations?

■ How can we avoid the practice of everyone for him- or herself? Without a Christian faith ethic shaping the behavior of people in a market economy, what will guard against greed taking over?

■ What should be the role of government in providing financial assistance to its citizens? in protecting consumers?

Option 3. The Global Economy

We need only look at the labels on our clothing to know that we participate in a global economy. In the exchange of goods and services between people from countries that differ markedly in economic power, evidence abounds of people suffering from unfair competition. To sort out some of the issues involved in global markets, discuss these questions:

■ What is our personal obligation to laborers abused by the global market?

■ How relevant to businesses relocating in economically disadvantaged nations are these words from Deuteronomy 24:14: "Do not take advantage of a hired man who is poor and needy"?

■ What's good about a global economy?

Module Two
Building Knowledge

Session 2: Materialism vs. Values

Session Focus

Our Christian values can help us resist the materialism of our culture.

Session Goals

Participants will

- describe how materialism conflicts with Christian values.
- recognize how advertising promotes materialism.
- learn to make consumer choices and financial decisions consistent with their values.

Session Brief

ACTIVITIES	MINUTES	MATERIALS
Building Community	5-10	
Welcome		Refreshments; display of advertisements, junk mail, and so on (see p. 53)
Prayer		
Spiritual Reflection	10-15	Bibles (one for each group member)
Application Activities		
Checking Progress	20	Participants' worksheets from Module One
Story (materialism)	5-10	Story: "An Indian Parable" (p. 55)
Discussion: Advertising	10-15	Display of advertisements from Welcome
		Handout (photocopy on bright-colored cardstock): "Consumer Caution Card" (p. 155)
Values Exercise	10	Strips of paper (ten for each group member)
Values Ranking	10	Handout (one photocopy for each participant): "These Values Are . . . To Me" (p. 156)
Values and Spending	10	Handout (one photocopy for each participant): "Values and $$" (p. 157)
Follow-up Activity	5	
Wrap-up	5	Transparency or photocopies: "Biblical Guidelines for Stewardship" (p. 129)
		Overhead projector

For the Leader

From the earliest European settlement of North America, immigrants struggled in the battle between money and morals. John Winthrop and the Puritans who arrived in New England in 1630 hoped to found a city pleasing to God that would be a model for Old England. Winthrop believed that God made a limitless variety of individuals to assure that "every man might have need of others," thus knitting humankind together "in the bond of brotherly affection." He believed that "society was a body of separate parts, love the only thing capable of holding the parts together, and togetherness the only means of survival." But no matter how much Winthrop desired that the colonists love one another, ". . . neither promises of paradise nor threats of damnation could obliterate self-love, so the most Winthrop could do was try to contain it by yoking private gain to public good wherever possible" (Patricia O'Toole, *Money and Morals in America*, Clarkson N. Potter Publishers, 1998, pp. 1-2, 17).

Winthrop's battle wages on. Today's society embraces the ideas of people such as Ayn Rand, whose novels celebrate the rational mind that is not held back by "anyone's opinions, threats, wishes, plans, or welfare" ("What Is Capitalism," *The Ayn Rand Reader*, Plume, 1999, p. 420). Rand describes capitalism, at its best and worst, as a materialism that rewards people for individual initiative. Everyone may choose his or her line of work, achieving and acquiring according to one's ambition and talent. Unchecked, the Rand brand of capitalism leads to rampant materialism, echoing the "greed is good" slogan of the '80s.

However, the inherent connotation of the word *greed* is negative. Most often, we think in terms of those who suffer at the hands of greed, such as those whose opportunities are limited because they don't bring money-making abilities to the market. But doesn't greed make victims of more than just the economically weak? Doesn't materialism control our North American culture? Has anyone, including Christians, escaped materialism's hold on our wallets and lifestyle? Author

Lee Knapp, writing about the personal impact of giving oneself to consumption, says:

> *I have lost my separate selfhood, or at least momentarily misplaced it. Instead of finding it in my rich family heritage, or in the gifts that have surfaced in me, or in the laughter of my children, I have gotten sidetracked by the consumer culture's claims that I am incomplete and needy. I think what is bad is being considered as, or considering ourselves as, nothing more than "economic beings."*
>
> —Lee Knapp, "Shopping for the Real Me," *Christianity Today*, November 15, 1999, p. 70.

Building Community

10 minutes

1. Before group members arrive, arrange a table display of advertisements from the Sunday paper, a collection of junk mail, insert cards from magazines, and so on. As participants arrive, start an informal conversation around your display about the amount of junk mail and advertising we receive. Bring others into the conversation as they arrive. Continue the conversation over refreshments.

HELP LINE

Printed advertising is generally word oriented. If some participants have low reading ability, record clips of advertisements and play the video as participants arrive. Focus your discussion on the number of minutes devoted to advertising in a 30-minute sitcom or a two-hour movie.

2. Call the group to your discussion area, and explain that you'll look closer at advertising and other aspects of our materialistic society during this session. Offer a brief prayer of thanks for the richness of our culture, and ask the Holy Spirit to shape each person's consumer values.

Spiritual Reflection

10-15 minutes

Once again we can find direction in God's Word for living in a materialistic culture. Read the selected passages aloud as participants follow along in their Bibles, or ask for volunteer readers.

> *Whoever loves money never has money enough; whoever loves*
> *wealth is never satisfied with his income. This too is meaningless.*
> —Ecclesiastes 5:10

The writer of Ecclesiastes notes that the pursuit of money leads to futility. This pursuer lives a life without purpose, promise, or progress. Putting an end to an aimless life—finding real value—comes from accepting the promises of God.

> *Then he [Jesus] said to them, "Watch out! Be on your guard against*
> *all types of greed; a man's life does not consist in the abundance of*
> *his possessions."*
> —Luke 12:15

Every one of us is selfish—money brings it out. We see evidence of a want for more, quite apart from happiness and fulfillment, in people of all races and all socioeconomic backgrounds. However, most people have little understanding of the effects of materialism on their lives.

*Jesus answered, "If you want to be perfect, go, sell your possessions
and give to the poor."*

—Matthew 19:21

Not everyone can take the attitude of George Washington Carver. When he
lost his entire life savings of $70,000 in the crash of an Alabama bank, he was
unperturbed. He said, "I guess somebody found a use for it. I was not using it
myself" (Clifton Fadiman, editor, *The Little, Brown Book of Anecdotes*, Little,
Brown and Company, 1985). Was Carver rich or poor?

When we put North American poverty in a global perspective, the poverty-
level income in North America would be a rich person's income in most developing countries. A $20,000 per year income ranks in the top two or three
percent income bracket in the world economy. Are we rich or poor?

*Why should I fear when evil days come, when wicked deceivers sur-
round me—those who trust in their wealth and brag of their great
riches? No man can redeem the life of another or give to God a ransom for him—the ransom for a life is costly, no payment is ever
enough—that he should live on forever and not see decay.*

—Psalm 49:5-9

When this passage from Psalm 49 was introduced at a *Faith and Finances*
field-test site in Chicago, a middle-aged man who had seemed bored with the
previous sessions quickly came alive. He said for him the "evil days" were pay-
days, when false friends showed up to share his paycheck. These friends were
interested in him only as long as he had "green" in his hands; they had no
appreciation for life and overestimated the value of money.

Materialism affects our relationships with others and with God. For many
people, money and things replace God. And it's ironic that this materialism
seems to result in poverty and debt. Rampant consumerism and materialism
often create rather than fill the void in people's lives.

Application Activities

Checking Progress

20 minutes

We've built in time this session for checking participants' progress on activities introduced in Module One. Most likely mentors will work one-on-one with their assigned group members during this time. These are the worksheets they'll want to discuss:

- **"Where Is My Money Going"**
  Participants are recording their purchases over a four-week period. By the next session they should be able to calculate how much they could save by cutting out unnecessary purchases.

- **"My Monthly Budget"**
  Participants are keeping track of their income and expenses for one month and estimating the amount they will spend next month. Perhaps they will make some changes in these estimates based on discussions about goals and values. Mentors will want to come back to this worksheet often during the next several weeks.

- **"My Financial Picture"**
  Mentors can use the "snapshot" evaluation at the end of this worksheet to help participants check their progress toward reaching new goals.

- **"My Financial Goals"**
  Particularly check progress toward reaching one or more short-term goals. Mentors will want to note problems and help participants find resources needed to get beyond these problems. Affirming every step of progress, no matter how small, is the most important thing the mentor can do.

Story: An Indian Parable

5-10 minutes

1. Children—and adults too—love stories. Read this Indian Parable aloud (or tell it dramatically if you're a storyteller) to introduce the concept of materialism.

   A guru had a disciple and was so pleased with the man's spiritual progress that he left him on his own. The man lived in a little mud hut. He lived simply, begging for his food. Each morning, after his devotions, the disciple washed his loincloth and hung it out to dry.

   One day, he came back to discover the loincloth torn and eaten by rats. He begged the villagers for another, and they gave it to him. But the rats ate that one, too. So he got himself a cat to take care of the rats. But now when he begged for his food he had to beg for milk for his cat as well. "This won't do," he thought. "I'll get a cow." So he got a cow and found he had to beg now for fodder. So he decided to till

Materialism . . . a preoc-
cupation with or stress
upon material rather
than intellectual or spiritual things.

—_Merriam Webster's
Collegiate Dictionary_,
10th edition, Merriam-
Webster, Inc., 1995,
p. 717.

_and plant the ground around his hut. But soon he found no time for
contemplation, so he hired servants to tend his farm. But overseeing
the labors became a chore, so he married to have a wife to help him.
After some time, the disciple became the wealthiest man in the village._

_The guru was traveling by there and stopped in. He was shocked to
see that where once stood a simple mud hut there now loomed a
palace surrounded by a vast estate, worked by many servants. "What
is the meaning of this?" he asked the disciple._

_"You won't believe this, sir," the man replied. "But there was no
other way I could keep my loincloth."_

—Mark Buchanan, "Trapped in the Cult of the Next Thing,"
Christianity Today, September 6, 1999, p. 66.
Used by permission of Mark Buchanan.

2. Ask the group this one question (probe until the group recognizes that this man got caught up in his things—in _materialism_):

■ **What happened to the disciple?**

"Just Get It!"

10-15 minutes

Our Western culture, urging us to spend money on things, suggests that our economic decisions are exempt from the guidelines we use in making decisions in other parts of our lives. "You are what you have" is the message that advertising promotes. The media says, "Go to the casino . . . take that cruise . . . buy the latest fashions . . . go out and party tonight—you deserve it!"

1. Distribute the advertisements from your table display so that each group member has at least one. Have them study the ads for a moment and find the slogan(s) that say "Just Get It!" in one way or another. Record these slogans on the chalkboard or newsprint.

2. Read the slogans back to the group—rapidly so that it begins to sound like a "noisy gong" that goes on and on. Discuss these questions:

   ■ **How conscious are you of this "noise" in the media?**
   ■ **What's the underlying theme of these slogans?**
   ■ **What needs are these ads aimed at?**

Emphasize that we all have basic needs—to belong, to feel secure, to be accepted, to be fulfilled, and so on. The market preys upon these emotional needs to sell products that can't begin to meet these deep needs of the human spirit. These needs can only be met when we are secure in our relationship with God, who lovingly provides for _all_ our needs—physical, emotional, intellectual, and spiritual!

   ■ **Does advertising target our sensitive and weak spots?**

Share the example from the Help Line on page 57 about the advertising of malt liquor to African-American neighborhoods where alcoholism might already be a problem. Look for other examples in your advertisement display.

While advertising claims to be sensitive to cultural and language distinctions, it often shamelessly targets the vulnerable. Here's one example:

> *A number of malt liquor brands are marketed most heavily in predominantly African-American, lower-income, urban neighborhoods using gangsta rap on black radio stations and displays featuring sexy, young African-American women. Critics are incensed because the alcohol content of these beverages is significantly higher than regular beer and because the 40-ounce bottles target a market with higher-than-average incidence of alcohol-related health problems. . . . [Such] targeting is the current darling of the marketing world.*
>
> —D. Kirk Davidson, "Targeting Is Innocent Until It Exploits the Vulnerable," *Marketing News,* September 11, 1995.

Notepad

Value . . . something intrinsically valued or desirable . . . to consider or rate highly.

—Merriam Webster's Collegiate Dictionary, 10th edition, Merriam-Webster, Inc., 1995, p. 1305.

■ **What can you do to fight the pressures of advertising?**

3. In response to the last question, distribute photocopies (use bright-colored cardstock) of the handout "Consumer Caution Card" (p. 155). Encourage participants to slip this card in their wallets and to "Just Say No!" to the pressures of advertising and materialism.

Where's My Heart?

10 minutes

1. Introduce the concept of values with this Scripture passage:

> *"Do not store up for yourselves treasures on earth. . . . But store up for yourselves treasures in heaven. . . . For where your treasure is, there your heart will be also."*
>
> —Matthew 6:19-21

2. Provide each group member (mentors and presenters too) with ten slips of paper. Ask them to write on each piece of paper one thing that they treasure (a possession, a person or place, an ability, a relationship, and so on). Then ask them to throw away all but one slip of paper. Ask these questions (don't probe for answers if group members aren't willing to share):

   ■ **What things do you treasure and consider of great value to you?**
   ■ **What one thing do you value most?**
   ■ **How difficult was it to choose this one thing over all the others you value?**

My Values Are . . .

10-15 minutes

—Exercise adapted from Karen Chan and others, *All My Money,* University of Illinois Cooperative Extension Service, 1997.

1. Distribute photocopies of the handout "These Values Are . . . to Me" (p. 156). Have each group member (mentors and presenters too) rank the fifteen values (just a sampling of values each person might hold) from lowest value to highest value.

2. Then ask these questions:

   - **What values did you rank very important? Was it difficult to choose these?**
   - **What values did you rank unimportant? Was it easier to choose these?**
   - **Are some of your values in conflict with each other? How about those marked somewhat important? Are some in conflict with what God's Word teaches about stewardship and money?**
   - **How do your values influence your goals? Do you want to change any of the short-term and long-term goals you set earlier?**

   Refer participants back to the worksheet "My Financial Goals" (p. 151).

HELP LINE

If participants seem reluctant to talk about their personal values with the entire group, have them discuss the questions with their mentors. This is a good way for the mentor to understand more about the participant's situation. (Mentors should also do the exercises and be willing to share their own values with the participants.) Be sensitive that not everyone in the group may hold the same values as you or the mentors do.

Values and Spending

10-15 minutes

Values influence our goals, our decisions, and our actions. Values influence the way we manage and spend our money.

1. Distribute photocopies of the handout "Values and $$" (p. 157). Work as a group to match the values listed at the top of the worksheet to the behaviors. Emphasize that each of these spending habits reflects a value—we don't make decisions in a vacuum.

2. If possible, allow time for each group member to identify the behaviors that match their own values or to reword the behavior description to more closely match their own values. For example, it's possible that someone values independence but would not pay high rent to live alone. This person could achieve a degree of independence by sharing an apartment, establishing a

corner of privacy for each person, and agreeing that each will do some things alone.

Here's the answer key for the values/behaviors match:

1. l. Simple lifestyle
2. i. Self-indulgence
3. f. Health
4. e. Fun, pleasure
5. o. Spirituality
6. g. Independence
7. m. Social justice
8. j. Self-worth, self-esteem
9. k. Service to others
10. n. Social status
11. c. Financial security
12. b. Family
13. d. Friends
14. a. Achievement
15. h. Integrity

(It's possible that more than one value will fit with some of the behaviors. For example, Claudie's behavior could also express self-worth, self-esteem.)

Follow-up Activity
5 minutes

We can finds signs of materialism and advertising that prey on our values right in our own homes. Encourage participants to check their closets, the bathroom, and so on for "walking billboards" (slogans, brand-name tags, and the like) that reflect our desire to be like Michael Jordan, to be accepted, to be in the know and in the lead. Or sit in a mall for a few minutes and observe the t-shirts with slogans, the brand-name shoes and jeans, and so on. Ponder what message the shoppers are giving with their "walking billboards."

Wrap-up

Show this transparency (or call attention to the handout) you used in the very first session: "Biblical Guidelines for Stewardship" (p. 129). Emphasize how these same principles can help us fight against materialism. Close with a brief prayer or a time of praise for God's amazing goodness and forgiveness.

Notepad

One of the questions asked in a nationwide survey conducted by the Washington-area public opinion research firms of Belden, Russonello & Steward and Research/Strategy/Management for AARP was this: What can money buy?

The 2366 respondents said

- freedom to choose (71%)
- excitement (68%)
- less stress (56%)
- peace of mind (47%)
- good health (34%)
- self-fulfillment (29%)
- family togetherness (23%)
- self-esteem (23%)
- happiness (19%)
- love (8%)

—Susan Jacoby, "The Allure of Money," *Modern Maturity*, July-August, 2000, p. 38.

If you omitted Getting Started, step 1, in Module One/Session 1 (p. 22), you may want to briefly introduce the concept of stewardship here (see also Alternate Program Plans, pp. 16-18). Explain that you will talk more about this topic later in the program.

Optional Activity

Use this optional activity to extend the session or to meet specific needs of those in your group.

Option 1. Real-life Villains or Heroes

We can find examples all around of us of people who have succumbed to the folly of materialism or of people whose love for God and others has influenced their financial decisions. Share the following stories with your group and discuss the values that prompted the behaviors.

■

Raft Goes for Broke

Actor George Raft made and lost millions. "Part of the loot went for gambling, part for horses, and part for women. The rest I spent foolishly," he said.

—Clifton Fadiman, editor, *The Little, Brown Book of Anecdotes*, Little, Brown and Company, 1985.

■

"Something Old, Something New"

Yuriza Madariaga knew exactly how she wanted to wear her long, dark hair for her wedding . . . but, there were two obstacles to the hairstyle of her dreams—her ears. . . . She broached the subject [of cosmetic surgery] with her doting fiance, . . . Christian Martinez. . . . "Anything you want," he told her.

The conversation got him to thinking. His nose, broken three times in falls and a baseball accident, had a noticeable bump. The breaks, he says, affected his sinuses, in turn producing frequent headaches.

"If you're going to get your ears fixed," he told his bride-to-be, "I'm going to get my nose fixed. . . ."

Total tab for the couple: slightly more than $12,000, which they are paying off over time. "We feel like it is an investment," says Martinez. . . .

—Abstracted from Kathleen Doheny, "Something Old, Something New," *The Grand Rapids Press*, November 25, 1999, p. B17.

■

Giving Others a Chance

Oseola McCarty, who before her death at age 91 drew nationwide attention, lived most of her life in a small, wood-frame house in Hattiesburg, Mississippi. She accumulated a savings from the money she earned washing and ironing clothes for others and then willed $150,000 to provide scholarships for financially needy students at Southern Mississippi. "McCarty said she wanted to give others the chance to get an education she never had. She had said she dreamed of becoming a nurse but had to drop out of elementary school to care for sick relatives."

—Abstracted from "Generous Donor, 91," *The Grand Rapids Press*, September 28, 1999.

■

Why Work?

Betty (not her real name) attended every session of the ten-week *Faith and Finances* program in Chicago. She was part of a job readiness and placement program and a prime candidate for employment. With her amiable people skills, she could do well in customer service. Yet, at the conclusion of the program, she had not found employment. When asked why, she replied, "I don't want to work. I'm living the life right now. I pay low rent, and I don't have to work. I sell candy and babysit to make some money—enough to get me by." (Betty is receiving Temporary Assistance for Needy Families—TANF—and qualifies for subsidized housing.)

—Erica Chung, MidAmerica Leadership Foundation.

Module Three
Changing Behavior

Session 1: Thrifty Living

Session 2: Risk Management

Session 3: Debt Management

Session 4: Home Ownership

Session 5: Investing

Module Focus
Learning new ways to manage money will help families build a secure financial future.

Module Three
Changing Behavior

Session 1: Thrifty Living

Session Focus

Thrifty living is an important step in the journey toward financial security.

Session Goals

Participants will

- describe what financial security means to them.
- identify the steps they can take toward becoming financially secure.
- analyze their spending habits to determine how to live more thriftily.

Session Brief

ACTIVITIES	MINUTES	MATERIALS
Building Community Welcome Discussion Prayer	10	 Refreshments Stories (see p. 66)
Spiritual Reflection Guest storyteller (optional)	10-15	Bibles (one for each group member) Simple tunic and sandals (optional)
Application Activities Financial Security— What Is it?	 10-15	 Chalkboard/chalk or newsprint/marker Handout: 　"My Financial Picture" (from Module One, Session 2) Transparency or photocopies: 　"Formula for Power" (p. 133) Overhead projector
Calculating Net Worth	10-15	Handouts: 　"What's My Power Worth?" (p. 159, one photocopy 　　for each participant) 　"My Financial Picture" (from Module One, Session 2) 　"My Financial Goals" (from Module One, Session 2) Calculators (optional)
Steps to Financial Security	15	Handout: 　"Where Is My Money Going?" (from Module One, 　　Session 1) Transparencies or photocopies: 　"Changing Behavior—Stepping Toward Financial 　　Security" (p. 134) 　"Keys for Financial Security" (p. 135)

ACTIVITIES	MINUTES	MATERIALS
The First Step: Thrifty Living	15	Markers (four), newsprint labeled with four expense categories (see p. 71)
Planning to Be Thrifty	20	Handouts (one photocopy for each participant): "Do I Really Need This—Or Do I Just Want It?" (p. 161) "Thrifty Tips" (p. 163)
Follow-up Activity	5-10	Handout (one photocopy for each participant): "Request for Credit Report" (p. 165)
Wrap-up	5	

For the Leader

How do individuals and families become financially healthy? Editors of the magazine *Black Enterprise* have identified these ten basic behaviors that empower families to achieve financial security:

- saving and investing ten to fifteen percent of after-tax income.
- learning about and becoming an investor.
- becoming a disciplined and knowledgeable consumer.
- measuring personal wealth by net worth, not income.
- engaging in sound budget, credit, and tax management practices.
- teaching business and financial principles to one's children.
- using a portion of personal wealth to strengthen one's neighborhood, faith, and community.
- supporting the creation and growth of profitable and competitive enterprises with a cause.
- maximizing earning power through a commitment to career development, technological literacy, and professional excellence.
- ensuring that wealth is passed on to future generations.

—Adapted from "Declaration of Financial Empowerment," *Black Enterprise*, January, 2000, p. 60.

These are sound behaviors for building a financially secure future. Approached from the biblical view of stewardship as we defined it in Module One, they're behaviors we can all endorse.

Building Community
10 minutes

1. Begin with a few minutes of informal visiting over refreshments. Then invite group members to your discussion area, and share one or both of the stories below with them. Ask the questions provided to introduce the concept of financial security.

■

Author Sherwood Anderson's publisher provided him a weekly check in advance with the hopes that he would be more productive when relieved of financial stress. After some weeks of this, Anderson refused a check. "It's no use," he said. "I find it impossible to work with security staring me in the face."

—Clifton Fadiman, editor, *The Little, Brown Book of Anecdotes*, Little, Brown and Company, 1985.

■ **What value is illustrated in this story?**
■ **Would you have taken the check? Why or why not?**

■

A cab driver tried to embarrass Lord Rothschild, founder of the London branch of famous financiers, about the size of the tip he gave. The cabbie said, "Your Lordship's son always gives me more." Lord Rothschild replied, "I dare say he does. He has a rich father— I don't!"

—Clifton Fadiman, editor, *The Little, Brown Book of Anecdotes*, Little, Brown and Company, 1985.

■ **Was Lord Rothschild's son "the last of the big spenders"?**
■ **Was Lord Rothschild tight or thrifty?**

■

2. Enjoy the discussion for a few minutes—you can learn a lot about your group members! Note that these stories illustrate that our values influence our financial decisions (Module Two, Session 2) and that financial security depends on how well we manage what comes in and what goes out of our wallets (Module 3). Offer a brief prayer thanking God for all that we receive and asking for wisdom to know how to manage our money.

Spiritual Reflection
10-15 minutes

1. As you consider the goal of financial security with your group, it's easy to lose track of God's view of wealth. Learning how to manage our money requires first of all a recognition that God gives us everything we need,

including the ability to manage our money. Begin your reflection time by reading to the group this reminder that God gave his covenant people:

You may say to yourself, "My power and the strength of my hands have produced [will produce] this wealth for me." But remember the Lord your God, for it is he who gives you the ability to produce wealth [obtain financial security].

—Deuteronomy 8:17-18

2. Jesus illustrated this tendency to rely on and credit our own power to obtain wealth with the story of the rich fool. Invite group members to read aloud or follow the story as recorded in Luke 12 in their Bibles.

HELP LINE

For a change of pace, invite your pastor or someone who enjoys drama to tell the parable of the rich fool. Provide a simple tunic and sandals. Narrate verses 13-15 to set the stage for the parable, and save the discussion until the entire story has been told.

Someone in the crowd said to him, "Teacher, tell my brother to divide the inheritance with me."
Jesus replied, "Man, who appointed me a judge or an arbiter between you?" Then he said to them, "Watch out! Be on your guard against all kinds of greed; a man's life does not consist in the abundance of his possessions" (vv. 13-15).

An inheritance seemed to offer financial security for this person from the crowd. Most of us probably cannot rely on that source of income to help us solve our financial problems. But notice that Jesus is more concerned with the underlying greedy desire for wealth than with the source of that wealth. It was this attitude that prompted Jesus to tell a parable.

"The ground of a certain rich man produced a good crop. He thought to himself, 'What shall I do? I have no place to store my crops.' Then he said, 'This is what I'll do. I will tear down my barns and build bigger ones, and there I will store all my grain and my goods. And I'll say to myself, "You have plenty of good things laid up for many years. Take life easy; eat, drink, and be merry"'" (vv. 16-19).

Sounds like good management, right? Obviously the man was a good farmer—who wouldn't credit him for increased yields? But what about his attitude, his pride? Notice the emphasis on *I*—no evidence of seeking God's guidance or of giving thanks to the Giver. Ease and pleasure became the values that drove the rich man's life.

"But God said to him, 'You fool! This very night your life will be demanded from you. Then who will get what you have prepared for yourself?' This is how it will be with anyone who stores up things for himself but is not rich toward God" (vv. 20-21).

This man forgot that he came into the world with nothing and that he would leave it the same way. Knowing God, our creator and our provider, is the only thing that will last for all eternity. It's all about values and attitudes. If acquiring wealth is our only goal, then we are poor. If managing our money so that we can serve God and others is our motive, then we are rich.

3. Serving God while managing our money is a goal impossible to achieve on our own. Conclude your reflection time with this passage:

> *The spirit God has bestowed upon us is not one that shrinks from danger! It is a spirit of action, of love, and of discipline.*

> —2 Timothy 1:7

We need to rely on God for our wealth and for wisdom to manage what God has given us. Embarking on this course of action requires that we overcome our guilt about past experiences and our fear of failure. Assuming greater responsibility for managing our money requires action (changing behavior), love (service to God and compassion for others), and discipline (sticking to a plan).

Application Activities

Financial Security—What Is It?

10-15 minutes

1. Recognize that financial security means different things to different people and at different times in our lives. Ask the group to describe what financial security means to them. Record their responses on the chalkboard or newsprint, and note the variety of responses. To some in your group, financial security may mean making ends meet; to others it might mean owning a home or saving for their children's education; to some it might mean saving for retirement or having enough to cover nursing home costs or to leave an estate for their children.

2. Ask participants to review the worksheet "My Financial Picture" they completed earlier (Module One/Session 2, p. 150). Focus particularly on the assets section of the worksheet as you introduce the following formula on the transparency (or handouts) "Formula for Power" (p. 133):

ASSETS	—	LIABILITIES	=	NET WORTH
(what you own)	(minus)	(what you owe)	(equals)	(power)

3. Ask the group these questions:

   ### ■ Why can net worth be described as power?

   Help participants see that net worth gives one the ability to act, to provide for future needs, to reach goals, to make decisions consistent with one's values. Net worth is the power needed to achieve financial security.

   ### ■ Which assets provide the most financial security because they appreciate (increase) in value? Which ones reduce financial security because they depreciate (decrease) in value?

   Record responses on the chalkboard or newsprint. Note that items that appreciate in value are *power* investments—they increase opportunities for financial security. Note that some items that depreciate may be essential expenditures because they help a person achieve more power in the long run. For example, an automobile may enable a person to get to work, earn a living, and eventually invest in a home that appreciates in value. The question then becomes, "What kind of automobile will do this?" Our values and our short-term and long-term goals will determine how we answer that question.

Notepad

One of the questions asked in a nationwide survey conducted by the Washington-area public opinion research firms of Belden, Russonello & Steward and Research/Strategy/Management for AARP was this: Why do you need money? Respondents gave these reasons:

- provide for my family (74%)
- get good medical attention (68%)
- stay healthy (64%)
- have more free time (34%)
- contribute to worthy causes (27%)
- buy more stuff (18%)
- travel (18%)

—Susan Jacoby, "The Allure of Money," *Modern Maturity*, July-August, 2000, pp. 34, 36.

Calculating Net Worth

10-15 minutes

Distribute the handout "What's My Power Worth?" (p. 159), and allow time for group participants to calculate their own net worth. (Provide calculators if you've been doing this in previous sessions.)

HELP LINE

It's best if participants can work one-on-one with their mentors to calculate their net worth. Note that the questions encourage participants to go back to worksheets you introduced in Module One/Session 2 ("My Financial Picture" and "My Financial Goals," pp. 150, 151) and to reevaluate their progress toward reaching their goals. If you discover that some in the group are struggling to bring the needed information about income and expenses, assets, and so on, encourage mentors to schedule an additional session with the participants. Even though the process can seem tedious, learning to keep track of their money is a big step toward making changes that can lead to financial security.

Steps to Financial Security

15 minutes

1. Ask participants to return to the worksheet "Where Is My Money Going?" (Module One/Session 1, p. 146). By now, they should have a fairly good idea of how much money they've saved by reducing what they spend on things they really don't need. Ask for volunteers to share the amounts they've saved and what items they've stopped purchasing. List the amounts and items on the chalkboard or newsprint.

HELP LINE

If participants have not completed the worksheet "Where Is My Money Going?" allow time for them to calculate their savings since they've started keeping track. If you haven't used the worksheet at all or if your time is short, simply ask participants to brainstorm a list of things they buy. Record responses on the chalkboard or newsprint, and then circle all those they think are *power* items—those that lead to financial security. How many purchases could have been eliminated at least part of the time? Were some purchases simply made on a whim rather than based on values and short-term and long-term goals?

2. Ask the entire group to pick any items on the list that they themselves simply could not live without. Circle any (hopefully few or none!) that are mentioned. Then have the group brainstorm ways they could use the money saved to meet short-term and long-term goals—to eventually increase net worth (power) and reach financial security. Note that it's still true that "a penny saved is a penny earned."

3. Affirm participants for their progress, and then introduce them to the steps toward financial security you will discuss during this and the next four sessions. Show the transparency (or handout) "Changing Behavior—Stepping Toward Financial Security" (p. 134) and briefly point out each of these steps (topics) you will discuss:

- **Thrifty Living**
- **Risk Management (Saving for Emergencies, Insurance)**
- **Debt Management (Borrowing and Credit)**
- **Home Ownership**
- **Investments (Retirement plans, stocks, bonds, mutual funds)**

4. Show the transparency (or handout) "Keys to Financial Security" (p. 135) and emphasize these three key words: *earning, yearning, learning*. Invite participants to share one time when one of these three key actions either added to or took away from their financial security. Emphasize how important learning how to manage one's money is to financial security—and it's a life-long process.

The First Step: Thrifty Living

15 minutes

1. If a person's goal is to set aside a certain amount of money every month to pay off a bill or to start investing, it's probably poor planning to count on a pay raise to make it happen. Ponder this dilemma by asking your group members these questions:

- **How likely is it that you can count on—with a high degree of certainty— an increase in income to meet short-term and long-term goals?**
- **If you are fairly certain of a raise, will the increase cover the rising costs of utilities, transportation, health care, and so on?**
- **If the answer to one or both of these questions is "no," how can anyone ever get ahead?**

Suggest that *thrifty living* is a good place to start. Acknowledge that participants have already identified some ways they can save money by cutting back on expenses for unnecessary items.

2. Ask the group if they think it's possible to be thrifty and still maintain a high quality of life. Divide your group (participants, mentors, and presenters) into four groups. Assign one of these expense categories to each group:

- **Food**
- **Clothing**
- **Utilities**
- **Entertainment**

Ask each group to brainstorm ideas for saving money in their assigned expense category. Give each group a marker and a sheet of newsprint labeled with the category. (If a group needs a bit of help, refer to the handout "Thrifty Tips," p. 163).

Notepad

It's been said that there are four ways to obtain wealth: steal it, inherit it, marry it, or earn it. The first brings trouble; the second may not happen soon enough, if ever; the third has no guarantees. That leaves just one way: earn it! Then learn to spend less than earned, and use the difference wisely.

3. Tape the sheets on the wall, and briefly note some of the ideas suggested. Take a survey on a few of the items, asking group members first if this is something they already do and then if it's something they would be willing to do.

Planning to Be Thrifty

20 minutes

1. It's easy to talk about being thrifty, but doing it takes thought and planning. Explain that thrifty living often comes down to deciding between *wants* and *needs.* Distribute the handouts "Do I Really Need This—Or Do I Just Want It?" and "Thrifty Tips" (pp. 161, 163). Invite participants to work with their mentors to sort out needs from wants and to identify ways to be thrifty. Provide catalogs, store fliers, and newspaper advertisements to help them figure costs, and remind participants to use the tips the group brainstormed earlier as well as those suggested on the handout.

2. Call the group together, and have each person share one way that they plan to be thrifty—to live below their *yearnings.* Invite them to bring a "show and/or tell" item or story to your next session, and allow time during that session for sharing about their thrifty living.

Follow-up Activity

5-10 minutes

A person's credit rating becomes an important part of his or her financial picture. In order for participants to have this information for the next several sessions, encourage them to request their credit report immediately. Distribute photocopies of the handout "Request for Credit Report" (p. 165), which gives directions for how to make this request.

HELP LINE

You may want to recommend *one* of the three credit agencies listed on the handout "Request of Credit Report." Trans Union will refer callers to a local agency, which may speed up the processing time. (Call this agency ahead of time to obtain the address, phone number, and fees of the agency in your area.) Some of your group members may qualify for a complimentary copy of their report (if they've been denied credit, employment, or insurance in the last sixty days or if they are welfare recipients); others will have to pay a fee. (Call Experian and Equifax ahead of time for the fee charged residents of your state.) Emphasize how important it is for group members to attach the requested documents. Allow eight to ten days for receipt of the report.

Wrap-up

5 minutes

Review procedures for next time and remind participants to keep bringing their folder with their worksheets. If you've been meeting for four weeks, those worksheets assigned in the first session should be nearing completion. Encourage mentors and participants to schedule an extra session if necessary to catch up anyone who is having some difficulty tracking the information needed. End with a brief prayer or time of praise for the richness of your lives and for the sense of community and caring developing within your group.

Optional Activities

Use these optional activities to extend the session or to meet specific needs of those in your group.

Option 1. Involving Families

Either as an in-class discussion or as a follow-up assignment, suggest that participants plan an activity that will engage the whole family in making decisions about thrifty living and saving. Begin by asking some of these questions:

- **If you are married, does your spouse share the same values and goals about spending as you do? If not, how will you compromise to build financial security?**
- **Did one or both of the marriage partners bring huge debts into the relationship? Are either or both of you uncomfortable with this debt? How will you arrive at a plan to repay the debt that will help you reach both short-term and long-term goals?**
- **Who assumes the major responsibility in your family for managing your money? Are you satisfied with this arrangement?**

Suggest that both partners need to know about good financial management even though one, because of interest or gifts or time available, might assume the task of day-to-day money management.

HELP LINE

Be sensitive to the fact that some members of your group may be separated or divorced and that financial matters may have played a part in the breakup of the relationship. Be equally sensitive to the responsibility single parents shoulder in managing their finances and the multitude of other matters for their family.

- **How can you teach thrifty living to your children? to preschoolers? to elementary-aged children? to teenagers? to young adults?**

Emphasize that modeling thrifty living and talking to children about the ways and the reasons to save money are important lessons. Even though younger children should not have to worry about their family's financial security, they can learn early that making ends meet requires everyone's help. Older

Notepad

Financial planner Allyson Lewis, author of *The Million Dollar Car and $250,000 Pizza* (Dearborn Trade, 2000) says that if $20 spent on pizza were invested weekly in a mutual fund with a 9 percent annual return, it'd be worth a quarter of a million dollars in 30 years. . . . Here's what [some other] seemingly small expenses would be worth after 20 years in a mutual fund earning 9 percent annual interest:

- Soda ($.75 per can, five times per week) = $7,280
- Lottery Tickets ($1 per ticket, five times per week) = $10,192
- Mocha Latte ($3 per grande, five times per week) = $43,682
- Movie Tickets ($20 per week for two tickets, popcorn, soda) = $53,207

—Ken Budd, "Small Change Is Big Money," *Modern Maturity*, July-August, 2000, p. 50.

children can be included in the decisions about where to cut back, what goals to set, and so on.

Option 2. Scenarios on Being Thrifty

To stimulate a lively discussion (and to get another look at participants' values and goals), present the scenarios below either to the entire group or to two smaller groups. Ask group members to decide what they would do in each situation and then to consider what a more thrifty person might do.

■

The Electric Bill

It's the middle of July, and you've just paid last month's electric bill. "It's way too high," you grumble as you hear the weather forecast for record heat the rest of the month. You have no air conditioning, and you're wondering how you'll ever sleep at night in this hot, sticky weather. Maybe . . .

■

The Prom Dress

Your daughter is a senior and has a date to the prom. She really wants the beautiful dress the two of you saw in the department store window last week. You've offered to give her $20 toward a dress, which will hardly buy the thread for the one she wants.

She could skip the prom or . . .

HELP LINE

When participants in the Bridge to Work program in Chicago were presented with these scenarios, their individual responses varied. They agreed that a thrifty person would buy a fan and take cold baths. They would turn on as few lights as possible and only have the fan running in the room they were using. One woman said she would not buy a used fan. "Fans aren't that expensive," she reasoned, "and I don't want what's keeping me cool breaking down."

The group was less united on the prom dress question. One woman in the group said she would "beg, borrow, or steal" to get the dress in the window! One said the girl should borrow a dress from a friend. Another said she refused to borrow clothes because "you just never know about some people's hygiene." She thought she might buy the dress on credit and *return* it after the prom.

—Erica Chung, MidAmerica Leadership Foundation

Module Three
Changing Behavior

Session 2: Risk Management

Session Focus
Good money management reduces the effects unexpected events can have on one's financial security.

Session Goals
Participants will

- describe risks or events that can threaten their financial security.
- realize the importance of saving for emergencies.
- understand how insurance can protect against risks.
- adjust their budgets to protect against unexpected risks.

Session Brief

ACTIVITIES	MINUTES	MATERIALS
Building Community Welcome Thrifty "Show and Tell" Circle Prayer	10-15	 Refreshments Chalkboard/chalk or newsprint/marker
Spiritual Reflection	10	Bibles (one for each group member)

Application Activities
Building Financial Security
	
	5-10
		Transparency or photocopies:
		    "Changing Behavior—Stepping Toward
		        Financial Security" (p. 134)
		Overhead projector

Events and Risks	15-20	Chalkboard/chalk or newsprint/marker
		Handout (one photocopy for each participant):
		    "What's My Risk?" (p. 167)
		Transparency or photocopies:
		    "Sample: What's My Risk?" (p. 136)
		    "Dealing with Risks" (p. 137)

Emergency Savings	15	Participants' worksheets from previous sessions (see list on p. 82) Transparency or photocopies: "Types of Savings" (p. 138)
Types of Insurance	15-20	Transparency or photocopies: "Four Common Types of Insurance" (p. 139)
Planning for Protection	10-15	Handout (one photocopy for each participant): "My Protection Plan" (p. 168)
Follow-up Activity	5-10	
Wrap-up	5	

For the Leader

That we live in uncertain times is probably an understatement. The newspapers and the media are full of accounts of devastation due to floods, tornadoes, hurricanes, forest fires—all natural disasters beyond human control. And there are wars and rumors of war, ups and downs in the global economy, inflation and recession, unemployment, and the list goes on. "Some, crushed by failure or hardened by pain, give up on life and hope and God; others, shaken, but still hoping for human triumph, work feverishly to realize their dreams" (*Our World Belongs to God: A Contemporary Testimony*, section 3, Study Version, CRC Publications, 1987, p. 15).

"Crushed . . . hardened . . . shaken"—perhaps these words describe those in financial distress. Some may have experienced generations of poverty while others may be reeling from the costly effects of divorce, death of a spouse, unemployment, illness, disability, or a decrease in family income. It's these families, discouraged and weighed down by the events in their lives, that most need to plan for financial security. But in reality,

> Families with very limited resources have little opportunity to put any plan into effect because current expenditures equal or exceed their current incomes. . . . Risks are minimized by Social Security, welfare, and other governmental and private insurance and support programs. Where individuals contribute or receive fringe benefits, the conditions whereby risks are covered are known and provide a base on which to build. Other programs are available in case contingencies cannot be met by individuals and families. With all available support taken into account, there is still

> a great need for families to consider how their particular risks and uncertainties can best be met.

—Ruth E. Deacon and Francille M. Firebaugh, *Family Resource Management: Principles and Applications*, 2nd edition, Allyn and Bacon, Inc., 1988, pp. 131-132.

Families who struggle financially may "give up on life and hope and God" or they may, "still hoping for human triumph, work feverishly to realize their dreams." This is where a faith-based program to help families manage their money can play a significant role. As participants learn specific decision making skills, they gain the perspective—perhaps for the first time—that God is in control of the events of our lives.

> God directs and bends to his will all that happens in his world.
> As history unfolds in ways we only know in part, all things—from crops to grades, from jobs to laws—are under his control.
> God is present in our world by his Word and Spirit.
> The faithfulness of our great Provider gives sense to our days and hope to our years.
> The future is secure, for our world belongs to God.
>
> —Our World Belongs to God, section 13

Building Community

10-15 minutes

1. Begin with a few minutes of informal visiting over refreshments. Then invite group members to your discussion area, and ask for volunteers to "show and/or tell" one way that they have been thrifty (see Planning to Be Thrifty, Module Three/Session 1, p. 72). You might want to record ideas on the chalkboard or newsprint. Ask each person to calculate the dollars or cents saved by their thrifty behavior, and then calculate the total amount of money saved by the group. Multiply this amount by weeks and years, and it's obvious the savings will add up.

HELP LINE

You might offer to type up the list of thrifty ideas your group members shared and bring it in handout form to your next session. This is a good way to validate participants' progress on their journey to financial security.

2. Affirm everyone for their good ideas. Invite group members to participate in a circle prayer expressing thanks for God's goodness and bringing specific requests to him.

HELP LINE

Before introducing a group prayer time, be sure participants are comfortable with this process. Assure them that it's OK to pray silently. If praying aloud seems like a stretch, ask group members to write their requests on a card so that you can pray for their needs either before the group or during the coming week.

Spiritual Reflection

10 minutes

Worry about the future and about financial security probably overtakes everyone at one time or another. Yet Jesus assured his disciples—and us—that we don't need to be overly anxious. Invite group members to read aloud or to follow as you read Jesus' words as recorded in Luke 12.

Then Jesus said to his disciples, "Therefore I tell you, do not worry about your life, what you will eat; or about your body, what you will wear. Life is more than food, and the body more than clothes. Consider the ravens: They do not sow or reap, they have no storeroom or barn; yet God feeds them. And how much more valuable you are than birds! Who of you by worrying can add a single hour to his life? Since you cannot do this very little thing, why do you worry about the rest? (vv. 22-26).

Notice that Jesus spoke these words to his disciples immediately after he told the parable of the rich fool (Luke 12:16-21). Jesus had warned the rich about coveting more riches, but now he warns those who have little of worldly goods not to worry or to want more. Jesus reminds his disciples that they are "valuable" and then asks a question: "Can anyone add an inch to their stature?" (You might have everyone stand to demonstrate the obvious answer.) It's obvious that worry doesn't accomplish anything, and yet we worry anyway.

> "Consider how the lilies grow. They do not labor or spin. Yet I tell you, not even Solomon in all his splendor was dressed like one of these. If that is how God clothes the grass of the field, which is here today, and tomorrow is thrown into the fire, how much more will he clothe you, O you of little faith! And do not set your heart on what you will eat or drink; do not worry about it. For the pagan world runs after all such things, and your Father knows that you need them. But seek his kingdom, and these things will be given to you as well" (vv. 27-31).

Worry is more than just a habit or a personality trait—it's a faith issue. If we really believe that God is all powerful and all knowing, then why do we worry? Is it because we don't trust God enough, or is it because we want what everyone else in our culture seems to want? It's probably some of both.

> "Do not be afraid, little flock, for your Father has been pleased to give you the kingdom. Sell your possessions and give to the poor. Provide purses for yourselves that will not wear out, a treasure in heaven that will not be exhausted, where no thief comes near and no moth destroys. For where your treasure is, there your heart will be also" (32-34).

We've reflected on this theme in previous sessions. We need first to be concerned for our souls and then to trust God with all our other affairs. James also puts planning for our financial security in focus with these words:

> Why, you do not even know what will happen tomorrow. What is your life? You are a mist that appears for a little while and then vanishes. Instead, you ought to say, "If it is the Lord's will, we will live and do this or that."
>
> —James 4:14-15

This is not an easy Scripture to apply. Are we not trusting God when we save for the future, when we plan for our children's education and other goals? These are complicated questions with no easy solutions. They beg for answers that place more than a monetary value on life. And they cause us to see that all of life—even our planning—is dependent on God.

Application Activities

Building Financial Security

5-10 minutes

1. We've talked about the steps on the journey to financial security in previous sessions. To review these steps, show the transparency (or handout) "Changing Behavior—Stepping Toward Financial Security" (p. 134) you introduced in Module Three/Session 1. Emphasize that one can't get to the top step without starting at the bottom.

HELP LINE

A good credit rating is essential for home ownership. As you point out this step on the transparency, remind participants about their request for their credit reports (see Follow-up Activity, Module Three/Session 1, p. 72). Ask participants to bring their reports to your next session.

2. Note these two key concepts you will discuss in this session:
   - saving for emergencies
   - protecting (insuring) against risks

Events and Risks

15-20 minutes

1. Invite group members to brainstorm a list of events that might happen to individuals and families that could threaten their financial security. Record their responses on the chalkboard or newsprint. Events could range from the breakdown of a major appliance to the death of a spouse. We've given you some information in the Help Line below to aid your discussion.

HELP LINE

Events are pertinent unexpected or low-probability occurrences that require action. They include

- unexpected occurrences that cause delays or adjustments in the flow of life but do not change it, and
- unexpected occurrences that change the direction of the flow of life.

Some known situations can become event-like. Though the birth of *one* child is anticipated, the birth of quintuplets has to be a challenging time. . . . Such "events" carry long-term commitments that are both rewarding and financially awesome.

Risk is the hazard or chance of a loss. From a family economic perspective [risks can be divided into two categories]:

- General economic risks are . . . those conditions in the economy beyond individual control. They affect large segments of the population and are caused by such pervasive conditions as price changes, including interest rates, and unemployment.
- Personal economic risks reflect hazards of individual events and are independent of general economic conditions. . . . [They] make people vulnerable to events that have potentially costly effects on resources: property losses, disability and illness expenses, premature retirement, and premature death.

—Deacon and Firebaugh, *Family Resource Mangement,* pp. 49, 66, 131-132.

2. Distribute photocopies of the handout "What's My Risk?" (p. 167). Ask mentors to work with their assigned participants to assess the losses (risks) each person might face if certain events were to occur. The vertical columns along the left and right side of the chart describe the extent of financial loss, and the horizontal columns at the top and bottom describe the probability that an event will occur. A completed chart might look something like this:

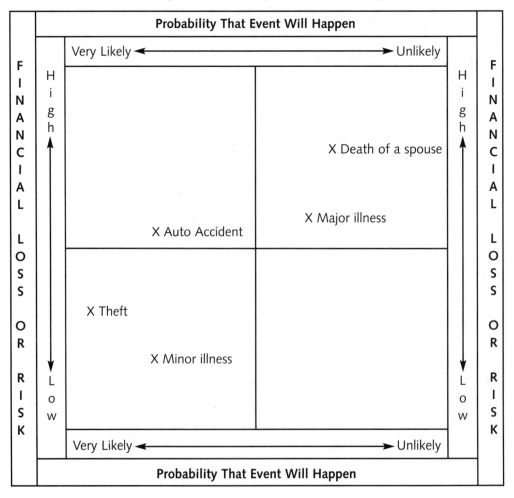

—Adapted from exercise developed by Karen Chan, University of Illinois Cooperative Extension Service, and presented at several *Faith and Finances* pilot test sites.

This sample shows that even though death of a spouse will only happen once, it can bring high financial loss (risk). An auto accident is likely to happen more often, but may carry less financial risk, depending on the value of the auto. A major illness may happen less often than an accident but could bring fairly high financial loss. Theft, depending on the neighborhood, may happen more often than an auto accident and produce considerable financial loss, depending on the value of one's personal property.

HELP LINE

It would be helpful to make a transparency (or handout) of the sample chart to show to participants and mentors before they complete the assignment. We've included an enlarged sample chart in the transparency section—see "Sample: What's My Risk?" (p. 136). Explain each example briefly to clarify the directions.

3. Emphasize that even though we can't predict when and if these events will happen in our lives, we can be reasonably sure that each of us will face some financial risk during our lifetime. How can we deal with these risks? To answer that question, show the transparency "Dealing with Risks" (p. 137), and discuss when each of these four ways might be appropriate (we've given one example for each below):

   ■ **Avoid risk by not putting yourself in a risky situation.**
   One might avoid lung cancer by not smoking.

   ■ **Reduce risk by taking measures to limit the probability or frequency of an event happening.**
   Theft might be prevented by locking all doors and windows.

   ■ **Bear the risk by paying for an unexpected loss out of your own pocket.**
   An appliance repair might be paid for with "piggy bank" savings.

   ■ **Transfer risk by purchasing insurance to cover a major part of the unexpected expense.**
   Supplemental health insurance covers some of the cost of medical expenses not covered by Medicare or Medicaid.

Emergency Savings

15 minutes

1. Show again the transparency "Changing Behavior—Stepping Toward Financial Security" (p. 134), and emphasize that saving for emergencies is part of managing money for a financially secure future. Ask participants to take another look at the handout they've just completed ("What's My Risk?"). Have them work with their mentors to answer these questions:

   ■ **What risks (losses) would you be willing to bear from your own pocket? (Have participants put a box around these events on the chart.)**

Notepad

According to a Merrill Lynch study of Census Bureau Data (cited in Peter G. Peterson, Social Insecurity), just under half (45 percent) of Americans are less than three months without income away from poverty; 78.9 percent of African-Americans, 72.5 percent of Hispanics, 67 percent of Americans under 35 years of age, and 79 percent of single-parent households lack savings sufficient to tide them over three months without a job.

—Universal Savings Accounts—A Route to National Economic Growth and Family Economic Security, Corporation for Enterprise Development (CFED), 1996, p. 9.

■ **How much money would it take to cover each one of these losses?** (Have participants estimate the loss, write the amount beside the boxed event, and total the amounts.)

■ **Where can you find money to start or build this emergency fund?** (Refer participants to these handouts: "Where Is My Money Going?" "My Monthly Budget," "My Financial Goals," "Do I Really Need This—Or Do I Just Want It?")

■ **Where will you "keep" this money?**

2. Give participants a chance to respond to the last question above, and then introduce the concept of *liquid* cash—cash that is readily available for emergency use. Show the transparency "Types of Savings" (p. 138) and briefly discuss each type.

HELP LINE

To aid your discussion, we've included a brief description of each type of savings in the Appendix—see "Savings Options" (p. 182). Some participants may not have a checking or savings account and may not know where to "keep" liquid cash or other types of savings. If so, briefly discuss these three types of government-regulated financial institutions:

• banks
• savings and loan associations
• credit unions

Banks and savings and loan associations are businesses that offer checking and savings accounts insured by the Federal Deposit Insurance Corporation (FDIC). Many of them also offer loans, credit cards, safe deposit boxes, and investment services. Credit unions are not-for-profit, member-owned cooperatives formed by people with a common interest. (For example, teachers in a local school district or employees of IBM or Allied Health may form a credit union.)

For people who need cash but do not have accounts at these institutions, checks can be cashed and money orders purchased at some businesses. (Because some of these businesses have a history of charging large fees, some states regulate the fees.) Post offices, grocery stores, wire services, finance companies, and pawn shops also sell money orders and cash checks.

Types of Insurance

15-20 minutes

1. Once again, show the transparency "Changing Behavior—Stepping Toward Financial Security" (p. 134), and emphasize that protection (insurance) against risks is the next step to financial security. Ask participants to take another look at the handout "What's My Risk?" they've just completed. Have them work with their mentors to answer these questions:

- **What risks (losses) could be transferred by purchasing insurance to cover a major part of the unexpected expense?** (Have participants circle these events on their charts.)
- **What insurance do you already have?** (Have them star the events/losses that are already insured.)
- **If you have insurance, do you know what kind of protection you have? If you don't have insurance for some or all of these circled events, where will the money come from to pay for these losses if they should occur?**

2. In response to the last question above, emphasize that insurance can protect us from devastating losses that we could not pay for ourselves. By paying a reasonable amount (a *premium*) on a regular basis, we can transfer some of these losses to an insurance company. Show the transparency "Four Common Types of Insurance" (p. 139), and briefly discuss each kind.

HELP LINE

To help with your discussion, we've provided some additional information about each of the four main types of insurance in the Appendix—see "Insurance—Protection Against Risks" (p. 184). If you find this information difficult to present, you might want to ask a family resource management specialist from your county or state Cooperative Extension Service to present this part of the session. (You'll find that this person will give a more non-biased explanation than an insurance agent.)

Planning for Protection

10-15 minutes

Have mentors work with assigned participants to draft a plan for protection against risks. Refer them back to the handout "What's My Risk?" (p. 167) and to the risks they circled that they could transfer to an insurance company. Then distribute photocopies of the handout "My Protection Plan" (p. 168), and encourage participants to work through the steps to develop a plan for managing risk.

HELP LINE

Participants will need to investigate insurance options available in order to complete the worksheet "My Protection Plan." If you or their mentors are comfortable doing so, recommend a trustworthy insurance agency they might visit. Suggest that they do some comparison shopping and report back to the group at your next session. Recommend that they do not purchase any insurance until they've discussed the options with their mentor or a knowledgeable family member or friend. You'll want to allow time for sharing this information at your next session.

Notepad

When participants in a pilot test session of *Faith and Finances* were asked if they had insurance for the most common types of coverage (property, auto, health, and life), no one in a group of 30 people had auto insurance. Risky!

—Gary Nederveld, MidAmerica Leadership Foundation.

Follow-up Activities
5-10 minutes

Encourage group members to visit one or more local banks, savings and loans, or credit unions to find out what options are available for saving emergency funds. Suggest they check interest rates, minimum balance requirements, and policies for withdrawal of funds for any or all of the types of savings accounts discussed in this session. Encourage them to open an emergency savings account if they don't already have one and are in a position to do so.

Wrap-up
5 minutes

Review procedures for next time, and remind participants to bring their credit report and their folder with their worksheets to your next session. Also remind them to complete their insurance protection plan by next week. (They'll want to contact one or more insurance agencies and be ready to share information.) Encourage mentors and participants to schedule an extra session if necessary to process the information discussed in this session and to continue tracking income and expenses (see worksheets for Modules One and Two). End with a brief prayer or time of praise, giving thanks for God's providing care through all the events of our lives.

Optional Activities

Use these optional activities to extend the session or to meet specific needs of those in your group.

Option 1: Checking and Savings Accounts

It's possible that some in your group do not have a checking account; others may need to know how to manage these accounts. Mentors can work one-to-one to help participants choose the best option for them (refer to "Savings Options," Appendix, p. 182) and provide support in setting up an account. Demonstrate the process of balancing a checkbook using a sample bank statement, cancelled checks, and deposit slips. Define the term *outstanding checks*. Explain how a carefully kept check register (show a sample that corresponds with sample bank statement) can serve as a record of expenses and as a helpful budgeting tool.

Option 2. Deductibles

Nearly every type of insurance, except life insurance, has some form of *deductible* clause. A deductible requires that the insured bear the initial costs up to a certain level. Perhaps you have to pay $100 for an auto repair before the insurance company "kicks in." Similarly, with health insurance you might have to pay the first $500 in health care costs during a year before insurance picks up additional costs. Generally, higher deductibles reduce premium costs, especially for homeowners and auto insurance.

1. Calculate the costs and benefits of a higher deductible, using the example illustrated below.

Insurance on a 1993 Chevrolet valued at approximately $2500	
Annual Premium	Deductible
$1000	$100
$800	$250
$600	$500

HELP LINE

You may want to draw the insurance chart on the chalkboard or newsprint (or make a transparency).

2. Discuss these questions:

   ■ Where is the largest savings in terms of premium?
   ■ Which would be the best option if the car was "totaled" in an accident?
   ■ How much risk would you be willing to assume with this auto if it were your primary work car? your teenage son's car?
   ■ What deductible would you choose?

Module Three
Changing Behavior

Session 3: Debt Management

Session Focus

When debt compounds, it can enslave individuals and families and destroy one's financial security.

Session Goals

Participants will

- understand the implications of buying on credit.
- identify the source of their credit problems.
- develop a plan to improve their credit rating.

Session Brief

ACTIVITIES	MINUTES	MATERIALS
Building Community Welcome Feedback Prayer	10-15	 Refreshments Chalkboard/chalk or newsprint/marker
Spiritual Reflection	10	Bibles (one for each group member)
Application Activities Follow-up (Insurance)	 10-15	 Handout: "My Protection Plan" (from Module Three, Session 2)
On Credit?	20-25	Advertising slogans, pictures of products, and so on from magazines and fliers (see Help Line, p. 90) Three sheets of newsprint labeled with Yes, No, Maybe; tape

Credit Reports	20-25	Participants' personal credit reports
		Handouts (one photocopy for each participant):
		   "My Credit History" (p. 169)
		   "More About Credit" (p. 171)
		Free brochures (optional—see Help Line, p. 94)

Follow-up Activity	10-15	
Wrap-up	10-15	Participants' worksheets from previous sessions (see list on pp. 94-95)

For the Leader

Thus far in this program, we've emphasized building financial security through careful budgeting and saving for the future. In this session, we'll introduce the concept of *dissaving*, using credit against anticipated future income. It's become a way of life for many in our North American culture.

Buying on credit can contribute to thinking that the "good life" is found in things, a value system we discussed in the session about materialism (Module Two, Session 2). Management experts describe the effects like this:

> Families who get into a process of taking on new obligations as older ones are paid off may be acquiring a habit of dissaving: living beyond their means. If income increases, the costs of the credit may seem inconsequential. A problem occurs when there are contingencies— such as one's job being at risk—that make the costs and payments problematical. For longer-term credit, there usually is collateral to protect the lender's interests—which also protects the borrower, particularly when prices are rising and the house or other item also increases in value. Difficulties arise when prices are going down. At times, not only the value of the collateral but the means of payment, earning power, may also be at risk.
>
> —Ruth E. Deacon and Francille M. Firebaugh, *Family Resource Management*, 2nd edition, Allyn and Bacon, Inc., 1988, pp. 121-122.

During the four-year period between 1993 and 1997, consumer credit increased by 56 percent, from $803 billion to $1.3 trillion. When such debt is out of balance with one's assets and earnings, the result is bankruptcy. In the United States, personal bankruptcies reached a record 1.4 million in 1998 (Christine Dugas, "Bankruptcy Judge Fears Reform Will Hurt Poor the Most," *USA Today*, June 3, 1999, p. 05B).

Perhaps Elisha's advice to the widow whose creditors were coming to take her two boys as slaves is still pertinent today:

> "Go, sell the oil and pay your debts. You and your sons can live on what is left."
>
> —2 Kings 4:7

You can encourage participants in this program to find enough money to pay off their debts— through thrifty living or by increasing earning opportunities—and begin to "live on what is left."

Building Community
10-15 minutes

1. Begin again with a few minutes of informal visiting over refreshments. Use this time to affirm participants, one-on-one, for sticking with the program.

2. Invite group members to your discussion area, and ask for volunteers to share one thing they've learned thus far about managing their money that is proving to be very helpful. Encourage participants to share their frustrations as well, and list their concerns, questions, and so forth on the chalkboard or newsprint. Promise that you or their mentors will try to find answers to their questions (printed resources, a name or phone number of someone who could help them, and so on).

HELP LINE

Participants may raise questions that you are at a loss to answer. Your local Cooperative Extension Service is generally part of a community network and may be able to refer you to agencies and programs that help families deal with a variety of issues. Or check your local phone book for a listing of government and community agencies that could offer support.

3. Express appreciation for the continuing willingness of group members to learn together and to support one another. Offer a prayer of thanks for God's goodness shown through the love of his people.

Spiritual Reflection
10 minutes

Debt is not a modern-day invention. Both the Old and New Testaments address the dangers of owing more than one can repay. Invite group members to read aloud or to follow along in their Bibles as you highlight several passages.

> *At the end of every seven years you must cancel debts. This is how it is to be done: Every creditor shall cancel the loan he has made to his fellow Israelite. He shall not require payment from his fellow Israelite or brother, because the LORD's time for canceling debts has been proclaimed.*
>
> —Deuteronomy 15:1-2

One wonders how this practice would play out in our consumer-oriented society. Would people accumulate debt without any intention of repaying? What impact would a Year of Jubilee (the seventh year referred to in this passage) have on current bankruptcy procedures that require records of bankruptcy to remain on a person's credit record for up to ten years? What difference would this make in the lives of those who have lost farms that had been in the family for generations?

Do not take a pair of millstones—not even the upper one—as security for a debt, because that would be taking a man's livelihood as security.

—Deuteronomy 24:6

Old Testament women used millstones to grind grain for flour and daily food. Accepting them as collateral could be compared to asking a farmer to promise grain that has yet to be planted and harvested—his very livelihood—as security for a farm operating loan. And yet that is precisely what happens every spring in rural communities. Then when draught or hail or winds or floods reduce or destroy the crops, the debt remains.

The rich rule over the poor, and the borrower is servant to the lender.

—Proverbs 22:7

The lender calls the shots. Or as someone put it in more humorous terms when complimented on his new car: "Yeah, the banker's in the back seat." So should one never borrow? In itself there is probably nothing wrong with credit or "buying on time," but the Bible is right in warning that it can lead to servitude. For those who do borrow, moderation would be a good general rule. Many people who have successfully built wealth have avoided all personal debt except for a home loan and perhaps a college education loan.

Give everyone what you owe him: If you owe taxes, pay taxes; if revenue, then revenue; if respect, then respect; if honor, then honor. Let no debt remain outstanding, except the continuing debt to love one another, for he who loves his fellowman has fulfilled the law.

—Romans 13:7-8

It is our Christian duty to pay what we owe and to work out to the best of our ability a way to clear up outstanding debts. The only debt that we can never repay in full is the debt we owe to love one another even as Christ loved us and gave himself for us.

Application Activities

Follow-up: Planning for Protection

10-15 minutes

1. During the last session participants began working on the handout "My Protection Plan" (p. 168). Invite them to share their plan with their mentor first to discuss any questions they have from their comparison shopping.

2. Then ask participants to share their shopping experience with the entire group. Note what events were most often listed as the number-one priority for insurance. To help group members see the need for continued planning for protection, discuss these questions:

   ■ **What surprised you most about shopping for insurance?**
   ■ **What choices did you have to make when trying to find a way to fit the cost for this insurance into your budget?**
   ■ **What other events do you feel are still presenting unprotected risks to your financial security?**
   ■ **What can you do next to reduce these risks?**

On Credit?

20-25 minutes

—Exercise adapted from Karen Chan and others, *All My Money*, University of Illinois Cooperative Extension Service, 1997.

1. "Buy now—pay later!" Ask group members to brainstorm a list of other similar slogans group members have heard ("no interest for six months," "no payments until next year," "no money down," and so on). Record their responses on the chalkboard or newsprint. Show the group the collection of slogans you've brought (see Help Line below), and add any to the list the group didn't mention.

2. Give each group member one or more pictures of items they might want to purchase (see Help Line below for ideas). Ask them if they would use credit to buy the item(s), and then have them answer the question by taping the pictures to one of three sheets of newsprint you've labeled "Yes," "No," and "Maybe." As they do so, have each person explain his or her answer. Check if everyone agrees, and allow time for a bit of disagreement, perhaps even moving some of the responses to a different sheet.

HELP LINE

Ahead of time, collect advertisements that promote purchasing on credit. Also clip pictures of products such as appliances, clothing, groceries, furniture, gasoline, medications, automobiles, and houses from magazines or fliers. Bring a picture of a cap and gown or a stack of books to represent an education and a picture of a family on vacation (or travel brochures). You'll want at least one picture for each group member.

3. Help participants sort through some of the mixed responses by asking these questions (possible answers follow each question):

■ **What are some advantages to using credit?**

Responses might include

- Credit allows families to use goods and services as they pay for them.
  Major appliances are often purchased on credit, but it's important to consider the life expectancy of an appliance compared to the number of years required to pay off the credit. Utilities are usually extended on a credit basis, but failure to pay these bills can quickly result in a poor credit rating.

- Credit gives families some flexibility in the way they use their income.
  Some families choose to use credit rather than dip into savings.

- Credit can be used to meet emergency expenses.
  However, unless expenses are reduced somewhere else or income is increased, this can lead to further trouble.

- Credit allows families to buy on sale.
  Purchasing something on sale with credit is wise only if any finance charge will not exceed the amount saved on the sale price. It's not wise to buy something on credit that will be "eaten soon," meaning it won't last a month or even a year.

- Credit can open opportunities to get ahead.
  For example, student loans allow a person to get an education and pay for it with earnings that are probably higher than if that person had not gone to vocational school or college.

- Credit can lead to increased wealth.
  A home mortgage will help a family build assets, provided the price of housing continues to rise. Purchasing on credit what will retain or increase in value is the best use of credit.

■ **What are some disadvantages to using credit?**

Responses might include

- Credit fosters materialistic values.
- Credit is repaid from future income, which may decrease.
- Even though much consumer credit is a short-term transaction, it can be used over longer periods of time, adding to the cost of the item purchased.
- Consumers get into the habit of borrowing and can easily overextend themselves.
- Consumer credit, when poorly managed, can lead to a poor credit rating and even to bankruptcy.

Notepad

Consider this scenario:

Credit card balance: $2500

Interest rate: 21 percent

Monthly payment: 2 percent of remaining balance

Time required to pay off balance: 63 years

Total interest charges: $14,699

—*Credit Card Smarts*, University of Illinois Cooperative Extension Service, 1998.

■ **Is it ever wise to deliberately create a debt?**

Yes, if someone needs to create a credit history, it might be wise to deliberately purchase something on credit, knowing that the debt can be paid off according to the terms and with little interest cost. Some people, such as young adults and women who have not had a credit history separate from their husband's, find themselves in a position where credit is denied because they've never established a credit history.

■ **Should a person use an ATM or other form of debit card instead of a credit card?**

Specially coded plastic cards can be used to withdraw cash or transfer funds from a person's bank account to the recipient's account in order to pay for goods and services. ATMs, one form of debit cards, make it easy to spend and easy to overspend. While interest charges on credit purchases can be avoided by paying in full by the next due date, most banks charge a fee for some or all ATM transactions.

■ **Isn't using a credit card OK if the balance is paid in full each month?**

Even with prompt payback, this rule is still true: With each *unplanned, unbudgeted* purchase, one is forced either to reduce spending somewhere else or to work harder for extra income.

Credit Reports

20-25 minutes

1. In Module Three, Session 1, participants were assigned the task of requesting a credit report (see Follow-up Activity, p. 72, and "Request for Credit Report" handout, p. 165). Briefly review the credit reporting process as described in the Help Line below.

HELP LINE

Most of the information in your credit report comes from companies you have credit with, such as banks, mortgage companies, department stores, finance companies, credit card issuers, and so on. Some information—bankruptcies, judgments, lawsuits, and tax liens—comes from the public records of various court systems.

Credit reporting agencies . . . are governed by the federal Fair Credit Reporting Act (FCRA) and companion state laws. The FCRA permits [agencies] to list positive information on your credit report indefinitely. In accordance with federal law, accurate negative information—such as a late payment or an account turned over to a collection agency—can remain on your credit report for seven years. However, bankruptcies can remain on your credit report for up to 10 years.

—"Dear Consumer" letter, Experian Information Solutions, Inc., 1999.

2. Recognize that a credit history can give a very negative picture of someone's financial situation. Ask the group to reflect on this question:

■ **What factors can cause a person's credit history to look bad, even to the point that he or she is denied credit?**

In addition to the influence of our materialistic culture, debt problems might stem from an event such as a medical crisis, a job loss or business failure, a problematic relationship resulting in family breakup, a lawsuit, or other catastrophic events. But a poor credit history can also be related to a pattern of behavior such as gambling, a habit of overspending, or an attitude about money and status that one needs to break.

3. Distribute photocopies of the handout "My Credit History" (p. 169), and allow ample time for mentors to work with their assigned participants to review their credit history—and to make plans to improve or repair it.

4. If participants are willing to share, make a list of ways to improve or repair one's credit history. Record responses on the chalkboard or newsprint. If participants don't mention them, suggest these two possibilities:

• Cut up all credit cards.
  This is probably a necessary step since continuing to charge will defeat any good intentions to reduce debt and to build a good credit history.

• Consolidate debts into a single payment.
  This may be a good plan *if* the interest rate will be lower than that paid on current debts and if the repayment plan is manageable.

HELP LINE

Depending on their needs, participants may appreciate the "walk beside me" help of their mentors in contacting creditors and repairing their credit history. Be sensitive to the fact that some in your group may feel very inadequate, even ashamed, to meet with a creditor who may appear to or actually be treating them rudely or even unfairly. This may be a time when your church's benevolent fund could serve as a bridge from crisis to recovery.

5. Distribute photocopies of the handout "More About Credit" (p. 171). Also take note of any questions participants have and additional help or information they need.

HELP LINE

The "More About Credit" handout lists a number of free pamphlets regarding the use of credit and tips for improving one's credit history. You may wish to request one or more copies of several of these references to show or send home with participants.

Notepad

A twelve-month study ending in March, 1999, reported that 39 percent of bankruptcies were filed by single women, compared to 28 percent for single men and 33 percent for married couples.

—Christine Dugas, "Women Rank 1st in Bankruptcy Filings," *USA Today*, June 21, 1999, p. 01A.

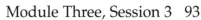

Follow-up Activity
10-15 minutes

If families are experiencing a debt crisis, repairing their credit history will require everyone's cooperation. Only in rare cases and with mature discernment might it be wise to leave a family member uninformed and out of the decision-making process.

Encourage participants to involve children and other adults in the process of repairing a credit history. While other family members won't necessarily be happier for this approach, they will be more likely to give cooperation and support. Teenagers especially will benefit from discussing how decisions about credit are made. Suggest these steps:

- Schedule a frank and open discussion of the situation when all family members are present.
- Outline what is required of each family member to correct the problem.
- Allow an opportunity for other members to suggest alternate ideas.
- Reach an agreement on a final plan of action.
- Agree on specific periodic checks on progress.

HELP LINE

Participants might find it helpful to role play a family conference. You can use the credit card scenario described in the Notepad on page 91 and ask for a volunteer to initiate a family discussion about paying off the $2500 balance. Or think of another scenario you've discussed as a group.

Wrap-up
10-15 minutes

1. Allow time at the end of this session for mentor/participant teams to look back over these worksheets from previous sessions:

   - "Where Is My Money Going?"
   - "My Monthly Budget"
   - "My Financial Picture"
   - "My Financial Goals"
   - "What's My Power Worth?"
   - "Do I Really Need This—Or Do I Just Want It?"
   - "What's My Risk?"
   - "My Protection Plan"

   Suggest that teams consider the participant's credit history and uninsured risks as they review current spending practices and short-term and long-term goals. Ask this question:

■ What changes may be required in the budget you are developing in order to improve your credit history? to protect against uninsured risks? to reach short- and long-term goals?

2. Once again affirm participants for their commitment toward financial security. Remind them that it won't happen overnight but that each step is one more on the journey. Close with a brief prayer or time of praise for a caring community and God's love in our lives.

Optional Activity

Use this optional activity to extend the session or to meet specific needs of those in your group.

Option 1. People and Countries

To present a broader perspective on the effects of debt, discuss how people with low incomes and high debt face problems very similar to those of poor countries in debt. Use the discussion starters below, and invite group members to contribute from their own experiences or from what they've read or heard about countries around the world.

• People with low incomes often owe someone else money. Countries with low incomes have bilateral debt—debt owed to another government.
• Poor people have little voice in money and banking policy. Poor countries have little voice in financial policies, terms, and conditions. A group of eight nations, including Canada and the United States, working with organizations such as the International Monetary Fund and The World Bank, make the loans and promote certain policies.
• People with low incomes and countries with low incomes have difficulty getting credit.
• Much of the income that poor people and poor countries generate goes to pay off debt, sometimes at the expense of providing for basic needs.

Module Three
Changing Behavior

Session 4: Home Ownership

Session Focus

Home ownership can have both emotional and financial benefits, but the question of affordability must be answered.

Session Goals

Participants will

- analyze their reasons for wanting to own a home.
- evaluate home ownership in relation to their present financial situation.
- investigate opportunities for home ownership in their communities.

Session Brief

ACTIVITIES	MINUTES	MATERIALS
Building Community Welcome "Home is where . . . " Prayer	15-20	Refreshments; Lincoln Logs, Tinker Toys, or Legos
Spiritual Reflection	10	Bibles (one for each group member)

Application Activities
Follow-up: Credit Reports
	10-15	Transparency or photocopies:
		    "Changing Behaviors—Stepping Toward Financial
		        Security" (p. 134)
		Overhead projector
		Handout:
		    "My Credit History" (from Module Three, Session 3)

Home—What Is It?	10-15	Chalkboard/chalk or newsprint/marker
Why Own?	10-15	Handout (one photocopy for each participant): "Why I Want to Own a Home" (p. 172)
Ready to Buy?	10-15	Handout (one photocopy for each participant): "Am I Ready to Buy a Home?" (p. 173)
Costs of Home Ownership	15	Transparency or photocopies: "The Cost of Home Ownership" (p. 141)
Follow-up Activity	5-10	Phone directory with yellow pages (one for each participant, optional)
Wrap-up	5	

For the Leader

Henry Ward Beecher once said that a home is "part of God's estate in the globe. . . . A parcel of ground is deeded to you, and you walk over it and call it your own. It seems as if you had come into partnership with the original proprietor of the earth" (Clifton Fadiman, editor, *The Little, Brown Book of Anecdotes,* Little, Brown and Company, 1985).

Home ownership is still the "American dream." Along with the pride of ownership, it gives families a sense of security and stability, peace of mind, and a feeling of permanence. However, this dream is not available to everyone. Probably in no other area of family finances are the gaps between rich and poor and between Caucasians and people of color more significant.

In spite of the years of prosperity our North American society has enjoyed, families with low incomes have not experienced the benefits of the economic boom. Working-poor renters find it increasingly difficult to find affordable homes or to come up with a down payment. Yet in many cases, these families will pay no more, perhaps even less, on their mortgage than they do for rent.

While homeownership for Caucasians tops 70 percent, homeownership for African-Americans and Hispanics barely hits 45 percent. In their book *Black Wealth/White Wealth* (Routledge, 1997, pp. 101, 104, 137), Melvin L. Oliver and Thomas M. Shapiro account for some of this disparity with these statistics:

- Even when earning $50,000 or more, African-Americans possess barely one-half the median net worth of their high-earning Caucasian counterparts.
- A $43,000 net worth situates a household smack in the middle of the Caucasian community's wealth distribution; but a household with the same net worth in the African-American community ranks among the wealthiest one-fifth.
- A small nest egg of $2,000 in net financial assets places an African-American household in the richest one-fifth of their community, whereas

the same amount puts a household in only the fortieth percentile among Caucasians.
- According to Federal Reserve Bank studies in 1991 and 1992, black and Hispanic applicants were denied mortgage loans two to three times more often than whites.

According to a National Community Reinvestment Coalition press release on the 1998 Home Mortgage Disclosure Act (HMDA) data, the percentage of conventional lending going to underserved populations is about half of their share of the nation's population. For example, African-Americans and Hispanics comprise 17 percent of the nation's households but receive only eight percent of all conventional mortgage loans. Native Americans and African-Americans are still being denied conventional mortgage loans twice as often as Caucasians, and Hispanics 1.5 times as often. African-American and Native American denial rates remain at 53 percent, the Hispanic denial rate stays at 38 percent, and Caucasians experience only a 25 percent denial rate.

On the bright side, *USA Today* (Maria Pvenke, "Another Boom Year for Home Building. More Minorities Buying, But Disparities Continue," June 21, 1999, p. 03A) reported that 1998 housing starts reached 1.6 million units. Mortgage interest rates and unemployment rates were at thirty-year lows. National home ownership hit a record 66.3 percent. Minorities accounted for 30 percent of first-time homebuyers, up from 19 percent in 1985.

Hopefully through your discussions and exercises this session, your participants will be encouraged that home ownership can be a reality for them—that it is a possibility worth working toward.

Building Community
15-20 minutes

1. Along with your usual refreshment area, set up a table with a pile of Lincoln Logs, Tinker Toys, Legos, or other similar toys. To add a bit of variety to these opening minutes and to introduce your topic for this session, invite group members to try their hand at building a house while they visit together.

2. Invite group members to your discussion area, and ask them to explain what this old saying means to them:

   ■ **Home is where the heart is.**

   No doubt, you'll hear a variety of answers—be sure to give yours too.

3. Then take a quick show-of-hands poll to see how many participants listed owning a home as one of their long-term goals (see "My Financial Goals" handout, Module One/Session 2, p. 151). Explain that you'll focus on the pros and cons of home ownership in this session. Offer a brief prayer of thanks for God's care in providing shelter and a place that each one can call "home."

HELP LINE

Be sensitive to the variety of housing alternatives participants in your group may be experiencing. Perhaps some already own a home but are struggling to keep up the payments. Others may just be dreaming of ownership while living in substandard or expensive rental units. Some may have been homeless at some point in their lives.

Spiritual Reflection
10 minutes

The Bible says very little about home ownership. When it does, it's often in the context of a place of security, as in this passage (have group members read aloud or follow along in their Bibles):

> *And I will provide a place for my people Israel and will plant them so that they can have a home of their own and no longer be disturbed.*
> —2 Samuel 7:10

God provides an immediate fulfillment to this promise by taking King David "from the pasture and from following the flock to be ruler over . . . Israel" (2 Sam. 7:8) so that God's people would once again have their own home (lands and houses) and be free from the persecution they suffered in Egypt. However, God also has a much broader intention: He promises in this passage to establish through David a royal house that will endure forever (vv. 11-16)—a promise fulfilled in Jesus Christ, who is preparing a place for us in his Father's house with many rooms (John 14:2).

> *Large crowds were traveling with Jesus, and turning to them he said: . . . "Suppose one of you wants to build a tower. Will he not first sit down and estimate the cost to see if he has enough money to complete it? For if he lays the foundation and is not able to finish it, everyone who sees it will ridicule him, saying, 'This fellow began to build and was not able to finish.'"*
>
> —Luke 14:25, 28-30

In some communities, dilapidated basements tell the story of people who began what they could not finish. In many overseas countries, homes may be under construction over long periods of time, but when a person accumulates a little more money, it's invested in the next stage of construction. One example shows short-sighted planning; the other shows planning toward reaching a long-term goal.

A MidAmerica Leadership Foundation board member buys and restores homes that have been lost by people unable to afford the mortgage payment and maintenance. After rehab, these homes return him a nice profit, a business he describes as "too good." "It's just sad," he says, "that people lose so much by not keeping up their home and their mortgage." We'll look at some of these issues later in this session.

> *Every prudent man acts out of knowledge, but a fool exposes his folly.*
>
> —Proverbs 13:16

We've been building knowledge about money management in this program—knowledge that everyone can use to achieve home ownership. It's foolish to think that our dreams can come true without having steady employment or other sources of income, without budgeting and spending wisely, without establishing a good credit rating or saving for a down payment. We can also falsely think that security is in owning property rather than being in tune with God.

Application Activities

Notepad

While home ownership is an important goal for Chicago families with low income, these factors indicate that the goal is difficult to achieve:

- The majority pay between 30 and 50 percent of their income for rental housing each month.
- Only about one-third of low income renters live in subsidized housing.
- A smaller but significant percentage still live in substandard housing or in over-crowded or doubled-up housing.

—Michael Wolfson and Brian Murphy, "Struggle to Pay Rent," *The Toronto Star*, November 6, 1999, p. A1 (based on a June, 1998, study by the Center on Budget and Policy Priorities, a Washington, D.C., research and advocacy organization).

Follow-up: Credit Reports
10-15 minutes

1. Show the transparency "Changing Behaviors—Stepping Toward Financial Security" (p. 134) you introduced in Module Three/Session 1. Emphasize again how important it is to

- provide for basic needs and save for emergencies (step 1).
- protect against risks through insurance (step 2).
- establish a good credit history (step 3).

   Point to the next step: real estate. One must establish a good credit history before taking this next step.

2. Allow time for mentor/participant teams to review the handout "My Credit History" (p. 169) you distributed during the last session (see p. 93). Have them review the chart listing bills due in the next two months and the plan to improve the participant's credit history. Then ask these questions:

   ■ **Will your credit rating qualify you for home ownership? If not, and this is your long-term goal, how long do you think it will take to improve your credit history?**

Home—What Is It?
10-15 minutes

1. To help group members describe the emotional aspects of owning a home, write these words on the chalkboard or newsprint:

- Home
- Homeless

   Then brainstorm all the words that describe each of these words. Most likely your list will reveal that a home is more than have a place to live—if that were the case, those without a home could be called "houseless." Homelessness also means a lack of security, safety, peace of mind, permanence, and stability. "Homeless" suggests loneliness and aloneness while "home" suggests togetherness and relationships. A home is more than a physical structure; when people move they adjust and feel at home again.

2. An elementary school teacher gives each of his students a rug that is considered "their place," a secure spot they can go to whenever they need it during their school day. This is their "home" at school. Invite group members to share "spots" they've claimed as their homes—their secure spots—over the years. It might have been a grandparent's kitchen, the farmhouse where they grew up, a quiet corner in their busy household, a park bench sheltered by a maple tree, an army barracks, and so on. Observe the emotional feelings connected to these spots.

Why Own?

10-15 minutes

1. Emotional benefits, such as those you've already discussed, are one reason for owning a home, but there are also financial payoffs. Distribute the handout "Why I Want to Own a Home" (p. 172), and give participants time to think about their own reasons for wanting to own a home. Have them discuss their reasons with their mentors or as an entire group.

2. Explain the tax benefits of home ownership, and discuss whether home ownership is really a protection against inflation in today's economy. We've given you a few discussion guidelines in the Help Line below.

HELP LINE

In the United States, both the mortgage interest and the property taxes assessed on a home can be deducted from federal and state income taxes—if the taxpayer itemizes deductions. Since most of the monthly mortgage payment for the first 15 to 20 years of a 30-year mortgage goes toward interest and taxes, even taxpayers who haven't itemized in the past are usually able to do so (provided their total itemized deductions on the federal 1040 Schedule A are more than the standard deduction applicable to their filing status).

Authors Gitman and Joehnk, analyzing the value of home ownership as an inflation hedge, state

> *"An* inflation hedge *is an investment that appreciates in value at a rate equal to or greater than the rate of inflation."* In the 1970s and 1980s, *"a home became one of the best investments you could make, since it generated a far better return than stocks, bonds, mutual funds, and so on . . . . Housing values fell sharply during the recession of the early 1990s. . . . Housing prices in most parts of the country [increased] at a rate about equal to or slightly above the rate of inflation. . . . Most experts believe that it will probably be a long time before we again see housing price increases that significantly outstrip the rate of inflation."*
>
> —Lawrence J. Gitman and Michael D. Joehnk, *Personal Financial Planning,* The Dryden Press, 1993, pp. 216-217. Reprinted by permission of the publisher.

Washington Post reporter Jane Bryant Quinn observed that in 2000, "mortgage rates and home prices are climbing in every part of the country [U.S.]" She notes these contrasting effects:

- [Many] buyers hardly seem to notice. They're confident about their jobs and earnings. Many are flush with equity in their existing homes or money taken out of stocks. First-timers can often get mortgages with little (or zero!) money down.
- But there's another side to this coin. Rising prices and rates are taking a toll on would-be buyers with lower incomes. The declines are especially notice-

able among single people, African-Americans, and Hispanic-Americans, according to the latest survey by Chicago Title.

—Jane Bryant Quinn, "Home Buyers Adjusting As Costs Build," *Chicago Tribune*, April 26, 2000, p. 5-3.

Ready to Buy?

10-15 minutes

1. Homes represent a major portion of the net worth of most North Americans. Each family needs to determine when and if they are ready to make this investment. Distribute the handout "Am I Ready to Buy a Home?" (p. 173), and allow time for mentor/participant teams to discuss the questions and calculate a readiness score.

2. If participants are willing to share, discuss these questions:

   ■ **What questions lowered your score (those that they answered "No" and scored a minus ten)? Why?**

   ■ **What one question are you least able to do anything to change? (Consumers have little control over the interest rates for home mortgages—but they can shop around for programs that offer lower rates.)**

   ■ **What one question do you need to work on most to improve your score? What will you do to make this happen?**

Costs of Home Ownership

15 minutes

1. The cost of home ownership never stops. Show the transparency "The Cost of Home Ownership" (p. 141) and discuss the six cost factors.

HELP LINE

To help with your discussion, we've provided some additional information about each of the six cost factors in the Appendix (p. 189). You might want to ask a loan officer from a local bank or a representative from a real estate loan program for low- to middle-income families to present this information. Make sure you've conveyed the specific needs of your participants to the presenter.

2. Allow time for participants to ask questions about the costs of home ownership, and record on the chalkboard or newsprint any that you or the presenter cannot answer. Promise that you or their mentor will try to find the needed information or a contact person by the next session.

3. To conclude your discussion, ask these questions:

   ■ **What causes homes to lose their value (depreciate)?**

   ■ **What can be done to encourage neighborhoods to improve and maintain the value of homes? Is this a bigger problem in neighborhoods with more minorities?**

■ Is home ownership a worthwhile investment or would you invest in something that might give a better return?

HELP LINE

This last question will give you some insight into the value participants place on owning a home and also their level of interest in learning about other investments—the topic for the next session. You'll want to look ahead to the Help Line on page 109 as you begin to plan for the next session and take into consideration the specific needs of your group.

Follow-up Activity
5-10 minutes

Have participants research special home ownership programs available in their area for families with low to moderate income. Suggest they start by contacting their bank or a real estate office. If you have time, have participants and mentors begin a search of the yellow pages in your local phone directory (key words: loans, mortgage, real estate).

HELP LINE

If participants are ready to make decisions about home ownership, it might be helpful for mentors to schedule another session(s) with them. Especially focus on programs that might be available for low- to middle-income families, first-time home buyers, and so on. Also consider programs like Habitat for Humanity. This is another time where participants will probably appreciate the "walk beside me" help mentors can offer. Make copies of "The Cost of Home Ownership" from the Appendix (p. 189) and encourage mentor/participant teams to use it as a guideline to evaluate the various options explored.

Wrap-up
5 minutes

Recognize that this session's focus may be both encouraging and discouraging to participants. Remind them that reaching a long-term goal such as owning a home takes time. Encourage each one to keep taking the steps on the journey to financial security. Review the procedures for the next session, particularly clarifying any follow-up assignments and handouts that need to be completed. Close your time together with prayer and praise.

Notepad

A location-efficient mortgage (LEM) program in Chicago factors in mortgage benefits for a home buyer who uses mass transit. A carless Chicago family of three earning $40,000 annually would qualify for a $151,000 location efficient mortgage (compared to $117,000 under a traditional mortgage). Benefits are greater in neighborhoods with better transit and nearby services.

—David Braver, "Wheel Estate," *Utne Reader*, July-August, 1999, p. 21.

Optional Activities

Use these optional activities to extend the session or to meet specific needs of those in your group.

Option 1. This Ol' House

To help participants better understand the costs of home ownership, select a low- to mid-priced house from the advertisements in your local newspaper. (Choose a house that would meet the needs of the majority of those in your group.) Ahead of time, contact a local realty office or bank loan department, and ask for their help in calculating the costs of owning this home. (Base the loan application factors on the average income, family size, neighborhood, work history, and so on represented in your group.) Include all six costs listed on the transparency "The Cost of Home Ownership" (p. 141) and explained in more detail in the Appendix (p. 189). Figure the initial down payment, mortgage points, and closing costs; calculate the PITI and maintenance and operating costs for the first year of ownership. Prepare a chart on newsprint, and present this information to the group along with an enlarged photocopy of the advertisement. Have mentor/participant teams decide if participants could afford to buy this house.

Option 2. Loan Application

Obtain copies of a loan application form from a local lender and have mentor/participant teams discuss and complete the form. (Participants may need to estimate some of the information requested.) This will help participants understand the value of record keeping, the need for a good credit rating, and the investigative nature of the lending process.

Module Three
Changing Behavior

Session 5: Investing

Session Focus

Since *how* we save can be as important as *how much* we save, we need to learn how to invest wisely.

Session Goals

Participants will

- understand the difference between saving and investing.
- describe the various types of investments.
- evaluate the degree of investment risk they are able to withstand.
- learn about socially responsible investing.

Session Brief

ACTIVITIES	MINUTES	MATERIALS
Building Community Welcome	10-15	Refreshments, display of real estate advertisements (see step 1 on p. 107)
Sharing Prayer		Home financing information
Spiritual Reflection	10-15	Bibles (one for each group member)
Application Activities Savings vs. Investments	10-15	Transparencies or photocopies: "Changing Behavior—Stepping Toward Financial Security" (p. 134) "Types of Savings" (p. 138) "Types of Investments" (p. 142) Overhead projector
Investing for Retirement	20-25	Transparency or photocopies: "Sources of Income for Retirement" (p. 143) Handout (one photocopy for each participant): "Am I Preparing for Retirement?" (p. 175)
Investment Options	15-20	
Return vs. Risk	15-20	Transparencies or photocopies: "Long-Term Investment Performance" (p. 144) "Take $1000 . . ." (p. 145) Handout (one photocopy for each participant): "How Much Risk Can I Take?" (p. 177)
Faith-based Investing	10	Handout (one photocopy for each participant): "What's Important to Me?" (p. 178)
Follow-up Activity	5	
Wrap-up	5	

For the Leader

Most of us do not set out to be millionaires. Neither did Anne Scheiber, but her life story would seem to contradict that.

While Anne Scheiber was alive, no one paid much attention to her. After all, she was just a frugal spinster living alone in a studio apartment in Manhattan. Her life seemed uneventful: she never took vacations or traveled, she never bought furniture, she never ate out, she didn't spend money on new clothes. In fact, neighbors claimed that when they saw her outside her apartment, which was rare, she always wore the same inexpensive black coat and hat. It wasn't until her death in 1995, at 101, that she received much notice. In her will, Anne Scheiber revealed that she had a $22 million fortune, almost all of which she bequeathed to Yeshiva University, a small New York University. This gift came as a huge surprise, not only because Scheiber had seemed poor for most of her life, but also because she hadn't attended Yeshiva, and, in fact, was totally unknown at the University.

Although the idea of a seemingly poor spinster leaving a fortune to an institution she'd never ever visited is fascinating, how Anne Scheiber amassed her fortune is even more interesting. She started out . . . working as an auditor for the IRS, earning $3150 per year. . . . When she retired in 1943, Scheiber invested her $5000 nest egg entirely in common stocks . . . the popular movie studios Universal and Paramount . . . soft drink companies Coca-Cola and PepsiCo . . . drug companies, including Bristol-Myers Squibb and Schering-Plough, both small companies at the time. Her stock dabblings continued throughout her life. . . . In the 42 years up to her death . . . , Anne Scheiber's stock holdings increased in value over 4,000-fold, making her a multimillionaire, even though she never lived like one. One of her best investments was the 1,000 shares of Schering-Plough she bought for $10,000 in 1950 and sold in 1994 for over $4 million.

—Arthur J. Keown, *Personal Finance: Turning Money into Wealth,* Prentice-Hall, Inc., 1998, pp. 444-445. Reprinted by permission of Prentice-Hall, Inc., Upper Saddle River, NJ.

Although we're probably not ready to live as frugally as Anne Scheiber, we can certainly learn from her generosity and consistent, patient investing in the future—a future she envisioned for others more than for herself. As we accumulate wealth through investing, God's Word offers both encouragement and warning:

In the house of the wise are stores of choice food and oil, but a foolish man devours all he has.

—Proverbs 21:20

Though your riches increase, do not set your heart on them.

—Psalm 62:10

Building Community
10-15 minutes

1. Along with your usual refreshment area, arrange a display of real estate advertisements either from the newspaper or from realtors in your area. (Make sure the homes advertised would be affordable to participants.) Encourage group members to browse and discuss prices, features, pros and cons of ownership, and so on regarding the homes.

2. Invite the group to your discussion area, and ask each participant to share one thing they learned from their research of special financing programs available to home buyers (see Follow-up Activity, Module Three/Session 4, p. 103). Record names and phone numbers of contact persons on the chalk-board or newsprint.

HELP LINE

Depending on the type of information about special financing programs participants bring to the group, consider developing a directory of the programs to give to the participants at your next session. Their collective research can be very helpful.

3. Express appreciation for the research each person has done. Offer a brief prayer of thanks for the spirit of love and community building within your group and for God's direction in each person's life.

Spiritual Reflection
10-15 minutes

The writer of Ecclesiastes weighs the meaning of riches in these words (invite group members to real aloud or follow along in their Bibles):

> *Whoever loves money never has money enough; whoever loves wealth is never satisfied with his income. This too is meaningless.*
> *As goods increase, so do those who consume them. And what benefit are they to the owner except to feast his eyes on them?*
> *Then I realized that it is good and proper for a man to eat and drink, and to find satisfaction in his toilsome labor under the sun during the few days of life God has given him—for this is his lot. Moreover, when God gives any man wealth and possessions and enables him to enjoy them, to accept his lot and be happy in his work—this is a gift of God. He seldom reflects on the days of his life, because God keeps him occupied with gladness of heart.*
>
> —Ecclesiastes 5:10-11, 18-20

To love money is meaningless. To recognize God as the giver of all we have brings happiness—both the things we have and happiness are gifts from God.

David, having learned this lesson well when he called for gifts for building the temple, offered this prayer of praise:

"Praise be to you, O LORD, God of our father Israel, from everlasting to everlasting. Yours, O LORD, is the greatness and the power and the glory and the majesty and the splendor, for everything in heaven and earth is yours. Yours, O LORD, is the kingdom; you are exalted as head over all. Wealth and honor come from you; you are the ruler of all things. In your hands are strength and power to exalt and give strength to all. Now, our God, we give you thanks, and praise your glorious name."

—1 Chronicles 29:11-13

Throughout Scripture we read of God investing in his people. God created everything, made a special bond with us, redeemed us after we fell, regenerates us with the Spirit, and promises us a place in the Kingdom. All of this, even the sending of Christ to earth, can be understood as God taking care of this investment. We in turn are to be God's stewards, managing the investment on God's behalf. We acknowledge that we fall short of living up to this.

The Confession

Most holy and merciful Father,
We confess to you and to one another,
  that [though you have made us and invested much time and many
    gifts in us,] we have sinned against you
  by what we have done,
  and by what we have left undone.
We have not loved you with our whole heart and mind and strength.
We have not fully loved our neighbors as ourselves.
We have not always had in us the mind of Christ.
You alone know how often we have grieved you
  by wasting your gifts,
  by wandering from your ways,
  by forgetting your love.
Forgive us, we pray you, most merciful Father,
  and free us from our sin [to serve you with the gifts you have given
    us].
Renew in us the grace and strength of your Holy Spirit,
  for the sake of Jesus Christ your Son, our Savior. Amen.

—"Service of Word and Sacrament," *Psalter Hymnal,* CRC Publications, 1987, p. 972.

Application Activities

This session on investing can be very intimidating to a participant who is struggling to make ends meet. If most of your group is just beginning to save for the future or considering buying a home, perhaps they are not ready for much more information at this point. We suggest that you use the first activity, Saving vs. Investing, to introduce participants to the next level of financial security and then the next activity, Saving/Investing for Retirement, to help them see the importance of starting now to plan for retirement. Then if some seem ready to go further, you may want to use a small group or mentoring to present more detailed information about investing. Those not interested would probably benefit from spending extra time with their mentors on topics covered in previous sessions. (See also "Alternate Program Plans" on pp. 16-18.)

Savings vs. Investments

10-15 minutes

1. Show the transparency or handout "Changing Behavior—Stepping Toward Financial Security" (p. 134) you introduced in Module Three, Session 1. Emphasize that

   - after spending for *basic needs* (step 1),
   - the less a family buys, the more they have to save for emergencies (step 1),
   - to purchase real estate (step 4),
   - and to meet future goals (step 5).

   Remind participants that protecting against risk (step 2) and establishing a good credit history (step 3) are ongoing essential tasks for building financial security.

2. Show the transparency "Types of Savings" (p. 138) you introduced in Module Three, Session 2. Review the types of savings listed, and remind participants that these savings are step one. Taking another step on our money management journey requires more knowledge.

3. Show the transparency "Types of Investments" (p. 142) and simply name the types of investments. Then discuss these questions:

   ### ■ How are savings different from investments?

   Refer to the definitions on both transparencies ("Types of Savings" and "Types of Investments"). Point out that money in savings is readily available (liquid cash), while money placed in investments is there for the long term. Savings do not protect one from the long-term risk of inflation that can decrease one's purchasing power. Investments seek to increase—but not so much protect—the initial investment. Although investments involve risk, they can be a way to build wealth over the long term.

■ **For what kinds of things would you use money from your savings? from your investments?**

Savings are good for emergencies, short-term uses, and as a preparation to make investments (for example, before buying a home). In general, investments are used to reach long-term goals (education, retirement, estate planning, and so on).

■ **Where are you in terms of building financial security? Are you saving for emergencies? ready to buy a home? saving for retirement? ready to invest?**

Answers to these questions will help you determine the needs within your group (see Help Line on p. 109 for suggestions about organizing the rest of this session).

Investing for Retirement

15-20 mintues

1. With the increase in life expectancy, most of us can expect to spend a considerable number of years in retirement. Although this may be a long way off for some, it's important to start saving and investing as early as possible. Once again, determine the experience of your participants by asking these questions:

   ■ **How many years have you been employed?**

   ■ **During these years, have you participated in an employer-sponsored retirement plan? If so, do you know how the money is invested and what the benefits will be when you retire?**

   ■ **Do you have a retirement plan of your own? If so, what type of plan?**

   ■ **Do you know what you can expect to earn in retirement benefits from Social Security (U.S.) or Old Age Security (Canada)?**

2. Show the transparency "Sources of Income for Retirement" (p. 143) and then distribute the handout "Am I Preparing for Retirement?" (p. 175). Allow time for mentor/participant teams to complete the chart, referring back to worksheets completed in previous sessions. In the Help Line below, we've included some additional discussion information about the five steps on the handout.

HELP LINE

Step 1. Under a 1983 U.S. law, the traditional retirement age of 65 will be raised in increments to age 67 by 2027. Beginning in 1999, participants in the U.S. receive an annual Personal Earnings and Benefit Estimate Statement (PEBES). An April, 2000, law repealed the restriction on earnings, permitting anyone from 65 through 69 to work as much as they want without losing part or all of their Social Security check. The repeal is retroactive to January 1. Social

Notepad

A 1993 study by Merrill Lynch showed that half of the families in the United States have less than $1,000 in net financial assets.

—Universal Savings Accounts—A Route to National Economic Growth and Family Economic Security, Corporation for Enterprise Development (CFED), 1996, p. 9.

Security benefits average about 40 percent of pre-retirement earnings. Persons with very low income may receive Supplemental Social Security benefits.

In Canada, the Old Age Security Pension (OAS) provides a guaranteed amount of income annually to every person over 65 and to financially dependent spouses over 60.

When persons receive only OAS and have very limited or no other income, they may be entitled to Old Age Assistance. These two major programs are not based on contributions; anyone who has been a resident or citizen of Canada for ten years is eligible. The Canada Pension Plan (CPP) is based on contributions, with a minimum ten-year contribution required.

Step 2. Most employers provide quarterly or annual benefit statements. It's important to know what happens to these plans if the employee leaves their job and also to check if a person is entitled to benefits from a spouse's plan.

Step 3. Employers may offer a 401(k) plan that allows employees to contribute a certain percentage of their wages which the employer may match. Taxes are deferred until retirement withdrawals are made when, most likely, the person's total income will be lower. Employees of schools and non-profit organizations may contribute to a similar 403(b) plan. Small business employees and those who are self-employed may contribute to a Keogh plan.

Step 4. U.S. taxpayers can contribute $2000 per year into an Individual Retirement Account (IRA) or a Roth IRA and delay paying taxes on investment earnings until retirement. If a person doesn't have a retirement plan or if income is below a certain amount, this contribution is tax deductible.

Canadian taxpayers can contribute to Registered Retirement Savings Plans (RRSP) that are tax-deferred investments.

Step 5. We'll cover this step in detail in the next activity. (See the Help Line below for ideas about organizing the next part of this session.)

Investment Options

15-20 minutes

1. Refer to the section "Some Investment Options" in the Appendix (p. 190). (You may want to photocopy this information for participants.) Discuss the key features of each of these forms of investments: common stock, preferred stock, bonds, mutual funds, and employer and individual retirement plans.

HELP LINE

It's likely that the majority of participants in this *Faith and Finances* program will be novice investors, if they invest at all. It's our intention to raise their awareness to some of the major options open to them without giving detailed information about each investment. You may decide to invite a broker or financial planner to speak to the group. Regardless of who presents, it's important that the information is not so complex as to overwhelm the participants and convince them that investing is beyond their reach. You'll want to leave them with the desire for more information before they make decisions about investing.

Notepad

Susan Jacoby, reporting for AARP, says:

A retirement confidence survey, co-sponsored by AARP and released at the end of 1999 by the Employee Benefit Research Institute, found that half of Americans have never tried to figure out exactly how much money they will need to maintain their standard of living in retirement. The same survey also revealed that more than three-quarters of all workers either think they will be eligible for full Social Security benefits sooner than they actually will or have no idea at all of when they will be eligible.

—Susan Jacoby, "The Allure of Money," *Modern Maturity*, July-August, 2000, p. 38.

2. To determine the experience level of participants, ask these questions:

■ **Have you invested in any of these types of investments in the past? What was your experience?**

Perhaps some in your group have tried investing and either did well or lost big. Some participants may have investment options through a retirement plan offered by their employer. Some have very little control over these funds; others must decide how their and/or their employer's contribution will be invested. Some may be investing in IRAs; others may be wondering if investing is a good idea for them.

■ **Are you in a position to start (or increase) investing in stocks, bonds, or mutual funds? in employer-sponsored or individual retirement plans?**

You might suggest that mentor/participant teams discuss this question together, reviewing worksheets from previous sessions to make a general determination.

■ **Whom would you rely on for advice about investing?**

Suggest that participants ask their family, friends, co-workers, or others who are experienced investors to recommend a broker or financial planner they trust. Most first-time investors are not ready to try this on their own.

Return vs. Risk

15-20 minutes

1. "The Dow Jones is up . . . the Dow is down. . . ." The attention given to the fluctuating market might make one wonder if under the mattress is the safest place for a nest egg. But there's more to the picture than what makes the nightly news. Show the transparency "Long-Term Investment Performance" (p. 144). Note that

- stocks in small and large caps have outperformed any other type of investment listed.
- every investment over the long term (1926-1998) has served as a hedge against inflation.

2. To further illustrate the long-term performance of various investments, show the transparency "Take $1000. . ." (p. 145). Once again note that stocks outperformed any other type of investment, and then focus on the advantages of long-term investing. Emphasize the importance of saving for a child's education, for retirement, and so on. The key is to start small but start now, as illustrated in the Help Line on page 113.

Notepad

A survey by the Investor Protection Trust, a non-profit organization that seeks to educate investors and investigate securities fraud, found that "fewer than one in five investors is 'financially literate'—meaning that they could answer basic questions on such topics as bond prices and interest rates, blue-chip stocks, and financial adviser background and credentials. . . . Of those who use a financial professional, either a broker or a planner, only about one in ten bothered to check the advisor's background."

—Albert B. Crenshaw, "Before Risking the Money, Invest in Financial Literacy," *The Washington Post*, May 19, 1996, p. H1.

Quiz participants before giving them the answers to the following questions.

- Investing $25 weekly for 40 years at a 7 percent average annual return will accumulate to

  a) $52,000
  b) $122,500
  c) $286,640

- Investing $50 weekly for 40 years at a 9 percent average annual return will accumulate to

  a) $239,400
  b) $644,500
  c) $1,026,853.

Answers: "c" is correct for both questions.

Notepad

"What will the market do?" a passerby once asked J. P. Morgan, a most successful investor on Wall Street.
"It will fluctuate," said Morgan.

—Clifton Fadiman, editor, *The Little, Brown Book of Anecdotes,* Little, Brown and Company, 1985.

3. Lest we all run out and buy stocks with the highest return, heed this advice investment companies often give: *Past performance of an investment does not guarantee its future performance.* Investing carries with it some degree of risk. The question we need to ask is this:

   ■ **How much risk are we willing to take in order to gain a return that will give us financial security and build wealth to meet long-term goals?**

   To help participants answer this question, distribute the handout "How Much Risk Can I Take?" (p. 177). Have them determine what level of investment best suits their willingness to take risks and still reaches their financial goals.

4. Then discuss this question:

   ■ **Would you put all your money in one type of investment or in several? Why?**

   The old adage "Don't put all your eggs in one basket" is good advice for investors. For example, when interest rates go up (as on Certificates of Deposit), bond returns go down. Having some money in each of these investments will balance gains and losses and reduce overall risk as the economy changes.

   ■ **How does time affect the choice of investments?**

   Review the rule of thumb on the handout. The more time one has to leave money in an investment, the more risk one can afford to take.

Faith-based Investing

10 minutes

1. We need to return to our discussion about materialism vs. values (Module Two, Session 2) when we consider investing. As investors, we want to get a

good return, but faith-based stewardship makes us also question how the returns are being earned. It's not just a "more-for-me" issue but also a matter of better living conditions and opportunities for others worldwide. To help group members (mentors and presenters too) sort through this issue, distribute photocopies of the handout "What's Important to Me?" (p. 178).

2. Ask for volunteers to share what they rated very important. Record their responses on the chalkboard or newsprint under the headings "Financial" and "Social." Then discuss this question:

■ **Would we be better off if we had laws that prohibited business practices that we know damage us, our communities, and our environment? Why or why not?**

Follow-up
5 minutes

Encourage participants who are or have been employed to investigate what retirement benefits they are entitled to under social security (U.S.) or Old Age Security (Canada) or from their employer.

Wrap-up
5 minutes

Recognize that no matter how hard you tried to keep this session low-key, some participants may be feeling overwhelmed or discouraged. Affirm the steps they've already taken toward financial security, and remind them that they've already come a long way. Encourage them to talk with their mentors about any questions that have arisen from this session.

Review procedures for your next (and last!) session, and clarify the follow-up assignments and handouts that must be completed. Close with a time of prayer and praise.

Optional Activities

Use these optional activities to extend the session or to meet specific needs of those in your group.

Option 1. Owning a Business
Entrepreneurs abound these days. Owning a business can be enticing, but investing in one's own business can also be a high risk. Many small business start-ups fail within a few years. To be successful, an entrepreneur needs a good business plan and must be willing to take risks and make the necessary commitments.

1. Share the story below with your group.

I was working in a mental health center some years ago when a family came in for counseling. They had never had much until Frank (not his real name) inherited a half-million dollars from his family. Instead of putting it into a safe investment, Frank saw this as the opportunity to become "really rich." He started a business. Each month the business required more investment, and within two years the entire inheritance was gone. Then a family that had been coping fairly well fell apart. Everyone was angry. Frank's wife and two daughters experienced his worst side, and he felt no support. The family, instead of enjoying the riches, lost its way, falling victim to materialism.

—Gary Nederveld, MidAmerica Leadership Foundation

2. Ask the group this question:

■ **What went wrong with Frank's investment?**

Frank was motivated as much by a desire to achieve higher status as by a desire to create an ongoing income. But he did not know the market or his competition, and he was not very realistic about his own abilities and his willingness to do the hard work required to launch a business. In a way, his inheritance was the sum total of his assets. He did not have the personal qualities and knowledge necessary to operate a business.

3. After discussing what went wrong in this situation, identify some steps Frank could have taken to preserve the inheritance—and possibly still have started a small business. Suggest that Frank might have asked for advice from sources such as these:

- a financial planner or broker.
- a local Chamber of Commerce.
- the Small Business Administration.
- local and national trade or professional associations.

Option 2. Investing Jargon

Some of your group members may be curious about the terms we hear frequently in the news media. Here are a few you might wish to discuss:

- Dow Jones Industrial Average (DJIA)
  The most widely followed measure of stock market performance; consists of 30 blue-chip stocks listed on the NYSE (New York Stock Exchange).

- NYSE Index
  An index of the performance of all stocks listed on the New York Stock Exchange.

- AMEX Index
  An index of the performance of all stocks listed on the American Stock Exchange.

- Standard & Poor's (S&P) Indexes
  Indexes compiled by Standard & Poor's Corporation; similar to the DJIA but employ different computation methods and consist of far more stocks; the popular S&P 500 composite index is based on 500 different stocks.

- NASDAQ Index

  An index supplied by the National Association of Securities Dealers Automated Quotation that tracts the performance of stocks traded in the OTC (Over the Counter) market.

- Bull Market

  A condition of the market normally associated with investor optimism, economic recovery, and government stimulus; characterized by generally rising securities prices.

- Bear Market

  A condition of the market typically associated with investor pessimism, economic slowdown, and government control; characterized by generally falling securities prices.

—Lawrence J. Gitman and Michael D. Joehnk, *Personal and Financial Planning*, The Dryden Press, 1993, pp. 555, 567, 569. Reprinted by permission of the publisher.

Option 3. Investment Clubs

If group members are interested and have sufficient knowledge about investing, you may wish to introduce the concept of investment clubs. This information is probably best presented as an additional session. We've included a brief session plan in the Appendix (p. 194).

Module Four

Giving Back

Module Focus

All that we have is a gift from God to be used in service to God and others.

Module Four
Giving Back

Session Focus

Giving back to God and to others in the community is an act of gratitude.

Session Goals

Participants will

- understand the reasons for giving back to God and to others.
- identify ways they can give of their time, talents, and treasures.
- realize that giving back builds up the community of faith.

Session Brief

ACTIVITIES	MINUTES	MATERIALS
Building Community	10-15	
Welcome		Refreshments
Evaluation		Suggestion box, notepaper
Prayer		
Spiritual Reflection	10	Bibles (one for each participant)
Application Activities		
Why Give?	10-15	Story (p. 122)
		Transparency or photocopies:
		"Biblical Guidelines for Stewardship" (p. 129)
		Overhead projector
How Can We Give?	15-20	Newsprint (4 sheets with phrases from p. 123), marker
		Paper (one sheet for each group member), pens/pencils
What Happens . . .?	10	
Wrap-up	30-40	Participants' worksheets from previous sessions
Follow-up Activity	5-10	

For the Leader

At one point in history, the church was the dominant authority in society, determining, for better or worse, what social justice was and who would receive it.

Good deeds were ordered by church authorities, leaders who held more power than anyone else.

Later, government was most dominant, especially in the socialist countries of Europe and Asia. Government leaders came to power promising to use the economy for the good of everyone. While their promises proved empty, they did lace society with an ethic for doing the common good.

More recently business has been dominant, and the classic economic ethic is doing what is in one's own self interest. Its proponents deliver a message that is gathering "true believers," and the church and government at best sing from the choir. Today government, in fact, is expected to reduce the barriers to a market economy in order to increase profits. Perhaps you've heard the saying "a rising tide floats all boats." This phrase is meant to justify a system that makes the rich richer on the assumption that it will also make the poor richer. But has our market-based economy done that? Or has it done irreparable damage to individuals and families, to communities, and to God's earth?

Star Parker, founder of the Coalition for Urban Renewal and Education (CURE), in describing ways to change the welfare system upon which she had been dependent, says:

> It is impossible to change the system without changing the minds, hearts, and spirits of those dependent upon it. Only God can do that.
>
> And through his power, churches and faith-based organizations can help. They can assist in reducing illegitimacy by emphasizing chastity before marriage. Through mentoring programs, they can assist in building post-welfare families. They can provide tutoring and literacy programs.

—Star Parker with Pamela Pearson Wong, "Breaking the Bonds," *Family Voice*, March/April, 2000, p.11.

Parker's words can be applied to our economic system and to all of society. God can change the minds and hearts and spirits of us all so that once again we recognize that the important things in life are priceless. Christians need to influence our present-day materialistic society for good, and we can do that best by being a model of service to others who lack opportunity.

Building Community

10-15 minutes

1. As you enjoy refreshments with your group, make a special effort to speak personally to each participant. Inquire about their families, their work, and other concerns they've shared over the past several weeks.

2. Spend a few minutes informally evaluating the *Faith and Finances* program. Bring a suggestion box and a stack of notepaper, and invite group members (mentors and presenters too) to write down ideas they have for improving the program or things they would have found helpful that either weren't done or could have been done differently. Then ask for volunteers to respond to these questions:

   - **What one thing that you've learned from this program has helped/will help you the most?**
   - **What one thing do you really need to learn more about or to practice more before you feel financially secure?**
   - **What one thing did you like best about this program?**

3. Offer a brief prayer of thanksgiving for each person involved in the program and for God's gifts to each one.

Spiritual Reflection

10 minutes

HELP LINE

If you haven't used the Scripture passages from Module One/Session 1 (see Alternate Program Plans, pp. 16-18), you may wish to use the passage from Matthew 14 for this session (see pp. 23-24) instead of—or along with—the passages below.

Once again invite group members to read aloud or to follow along in their Bibles as you reflect on the biblical view of stewardship.

> *As he looked up, Jesus saw the rich putting their gifts into the temple treasury. He also saw a poor widow put in two very small copper coins. "I tell you the truth," he said, "this poor widow has put in more than all the others. All these people gave their gifts out of their wealth; but she out of her poverty put in all she had to live on."*

> —Luke 21:1-4

It's not how much we have that matters to God; it's how much we're willing to give from what God has given us that demonstrates true giving back. The widow gave all—a sign of her trust in God and her generosity toward others.

If anyone has material possessions and sees his brother in need but has no pity on him, how can the love of God be in him? Dear children, let us not love with words or tongue but with actions and in truth.

—1 John 3:17-18

Talking about the homeless and hungry while enjoying our warm homes and plentiful meals does little good. It's when we reach for our wallets or use our time and energy to "do whatever . . . for one of the least of these brothers of mine" (Matt. 26:30) that we're truly serving Jesus, God's Son, who gave his all for us.

One man gives freely, yet gains even more; another withholds unduly, but comes to poverty. A generous man will prosper; he who refreshes others will himself be refreshed.

—Proverbs 11:24-25

"We cannot outgive God! It is more blessed to give than to receive." We've probably all heard these words many times, but it's when we really do "give freely" that we are "refreshed." Giving back is up to us; God will take care of the rest. That's God's promise to us.

"Test me in this," says the Lord Almighty, "and see if I will not throw open the floodgates of heaven and pour out so much blessing that you will not have room enough for it."

—Malachi 3:7

Application Activities

Why Give?

10-15 minutes

1. Perhaps no other story in the Bible, in so few words, teaches us about giving as does the story of the widow's mite (Luke 21:2-4). Jesus said, "She out of her poverty put in all that she had to live on." Jesus would have said that a little girl named Hattie May Wiatt also "gave all that she had." Read her story aloud to your group.

The History of Fifty-Seven Cents
Sermon by Russell H. Conwell
Sunday Morning, December 1, 1912

Little Hattie May Wiatt lived near . . . a small [crowded] church [in Philadelphia]. . . . The Sunday school was as crowded as the rest of the congregation, and one day . . . I found a number of children outside. They were greatly disturbed because they could not get in, . . . and little Hattie May Wiatt . . . was standing by the gate, hesitating whether to go back home or wait and try to get in later. I took her up in my arms, lifted her to my shoulder, and then . . . carried her through the crowd in the hall, into the Sunday school room. . . .

The next that I heard . . . was that Hattie was very sick, and they [her parents] asked me to come and see the child. . . . I walked up the street, praying for the little girl's recovery, and yet all the time with the conviction that it was not to be.

Hattie May Wiatt died. She had gathered 57 cents . . . as her contribution towards securing another building for the children. After the funeral the mother handed me the little bag with the gathered 57 cents. I took it to the church and stated that we had the first gift toward the new Sunday school building. . . . I then changed all the money into pennies and offered them for sale. I received about $250 for the 57 pennies; and 54 of those cents were returned to me. . . . [It was] money enough to buy the next house north of the church. . . . That house was bought by the Wiatt Mite Society, which was organized for the purpose of taking the 57 cents and enlarging on them sufficiently to buy the property for the Primary Department of the Sunday school. . . .

Then when the crowd became so great . . . the conviction was strong that we ought to build a larger church . . . "on Broad Street somewhere.". . . I walked over to see Mr. Baird . . . and asked him what he wanted for this lot on which the Temple now stands. He said that he wanted $30,000. I told him that we had only 54 cents.

[Later] Mr. Baird said, "I've been thinking this matter over and have made up my mind I will sell you the lot for $25,000, taking $5000 less than I think it is worth, and I will take the 54 cents as the first payment. . . . Thus we bought the lot, and thus encouraged by

Notepad

When you're in the city of Philadelphia, visit The Baptist Temple, with a seating capacity of 3300, and Temple University, where thousands of students are trained. Have a look too at the Temple University Hospital (formerly the Good Samaritan Hospital) and at a Sunday school building which houses hundreds of children, so that no child in the area will ever need to be turned away from Sunday school. In one of the rooms of this building you'll find the picture of the little girl whose 57 cents, so sacrificially saved, made such remarkable history. Alongside of it is a portrait of her kind pastor, Dr. Russell H. Conwell.

God step by step, we went on constructing this building. We owed $109,000 when it was done. . . . We could hardly have dreamed then that in the number of years that followed this, people, without wealth, each giving only as he could afford from his earnings, could have paid off so great a debt. . . . The only outside help that we really received was from Mr. Buckness. . . . He gave us $10,000 on the condition that we call this building by some other name than the Grace Baptist Church, and that accounts for its being called The Temple. . . . I must state here also that in the house purchased by the sale of the 57 cents was organized The Temple University.

[Hattie May Wiatt] was a schoolgirl . . . yet think how her life was used. . . . Think of this large church; think of the membership added to it—over 5600—since that time. . . . Think of the Sabbath school carried on this great building for more than twenty years. Think of the institutions this church founded [Samaritan Hospital, Garretson Hospital, Temple University]. . . . Hattie May Wiatt was being used to do a mighty work. . . . The humblest of his Christian servants is doing just as much for his kingdom . . . doing faithfully their little duty, as are the seemingly great. . . .

—Excerpted from the publication of the sermon in *The Temple Review*, the weekly magazine of the Baptist Temple, v. 21, no. 7, December 19, 1912. Conwellana—Templana Collection/University Archives, Temple University Libraries, August, 1997. Used by permission of Frederick O. Lewis, Minister, The Baptist Temple. (For a complete transcript of this sermon visit http://www.library.temple.edu/speccoll/hattie.htm.)

2. Reemphasize the concept of stewardship as you discuss these questions:

- **What lessons does Hattie May Wiatt teach us?**
- **How does this story illustrate God's opening the "floodgates of heaven"?**
- **What good things could happen in your church or community if each person gave "57 cents" worth of time, talent, and treasure?**

3. Show the transparency "Biblical Guidelines for Stewardship" (p. 129) that you introduced in Module One/Session 1. Reflect on how these three principles are illustrated in the story about the little girl.

How Can We Give?

15-20 minutes

1. Ahead of time write these four phrases on separate sheets of newsprint:

- Time (volunteering our time to serve God by serving others)
- Talents (using our abilities to serve God and others)
- Treasures (giving our money and material goods for God's work and to those in need)
- Trees (living simply and caring for the earth's resources)

Notepad

Stewardship from Two Points of View

- Challenged by a socialist about the injustice of his great wealth, Andrew Carnegie asked his secretary to do a calculation, dividing the estimate of the world's population into the estimate of Carnegie's wealth. Then he told his secretary to give the man his share—sixteen cents!

—Clifton Fadiman, *The Little, Brown Book of Anecdotes*, Little, Brown and Company, 1985.

- Kahill Gibran once said, "Money is like love; it kills slowly and painfully the one who withholds it, and it enlivens the other who turns it upon his fellow men."

—Kahlil Gibran, edited by Martin L. Wolf and others, *The Treasured Writings of Kahlil Gibran*, Castle Books, 1998.

Ask group members to brainstorm all the ways we can give back to God. Write their responses under one of the four categories.

2. Give each group member (mentors and presenters too) a sheet of paper, and ask them to fold it into fourths. Have them write one of the four "T" words in each quarter and then write down at least one way in each box that they will commit to giving back to God and others in the next week. If you have time, ask for volunteers to share the one they think will be the hardest to accomplish and why.

What Happens When We Give Back?

10 minutes

1. Review again what happened at The Baptist Temple when a little girl taught a lesson about giving back. With the group, calculate this scenario:

   ■ **Suppose that 3300 people attended church this past Sunday and that 1000 church and community children attended Sunday School. Multiply that times 52 weeks in a year, times approximately 80 years (about the time when the church was built). If each child brought 57 cents . . . and shared his or her time and talents—it's mind boggling!**

2. Ask for volunteers to share a time when they were the recipients of a much-needed gift or a time when they were able to give to someone in need of their time, talents, or treasures. Discuss these questions:

   ■ **In either case, how did the recipient respond? What feelings were expressed?**

   Feelings of joy, gratitude, reluctance, humility, and so on can be expressed when giving or receiving a much needed gift.

   ■ **What happened as a result of this gift?**

   Although changes may not be observable, lives have been changed because someone took the time to care about another person and to demonstrate the love of God. Perhaps members of your group have participated in or been the recipient of a Homes for Humanity project or other gestures of good will. Others may have been touched by a visit from a virtual stranger when they were hospitalized. God uses these gifts to work out his will in people's lives, blessing individuals, families, and communities.

3. Conclude your discussion of stewardship by asking the group to picture Mother Teresa in their minds. This dedicated servant of God was able to see God in the people she served; all the filters of class, race, social and economic status disappeared. That is God giving once again even as we give back!

Wrap-up
30-40 minutes

HELP LINE

You'll note that we've switched the wrap-up and follow-up times around for this session, assuming that this will be your last session. You'll want to bring some sense of closure to the program at this point. Perhaps you'll want to have a social time at the end of the session as well as at the beginning, celebrating the community of faith you've become and the accomplishments of the participants.

Allow sufficient time for mentor/participant teams to work on tasks they've begun (budgeting, managing a checking account, repairing a credit history, applying for a home loan, and so on). Remind group members to add their comments about the program to the suggestion box you introduced earlier in the session.

Follow-up Activity
5-10 minutes

Depending on the needs of your group, you may wish to plan additional group or mentoring/participant sessions. Perhaps there are topics that some in the group want to learn more about or that require additional help from a mentor (investing, buying a home, and so on). Plan in advance how you will work out these details, and decide how you and your church will keep in contact with the participants. Make sure participants leave with some sense that you will keep in touch, especially if they are not members of your church.

Optional Activity

Option 1. A Steward Is . . .
If you chose to adapt your program as we suggested in "Alternative Program Plans" (pp. 16-18), you may wish to use the activity "A Steward Is . . ." (Module One/Session 1, p. 25) to introduce the concept of faith-based stewardship. If your time is limited, use it in place of one of the activities suggested for this session.

Notepad

A Michigan study noted a side of giving often overlooked when schools teach about our economic system. For example, few texts or teachers discuss

- the 13 percent of the economy represented in the activities of the non-profit sector.
- the 20 billion volunteer hours each year that add value to the economy and promote our common community interests.

—*For the Common Good*, The Council of Michigan Foundations, from their web site: www.msu.edu/~k12phil

Reproducible Resources

Transparency Masters

Handouts

Module One

Module Two

Module Three

Biblical Guidelines for Stewardship

- All of life is a gift from God.

- Our sins damage and even destroy some of this gift.

- The world is not *mine* but *ours*.

Faith and Finances: A Brief Overview

Changing
Behavior

FINANCIAL SECURITY

Giving Back

Investing

Home Ownership

Debt Management

Risk Management

Thrifty Living

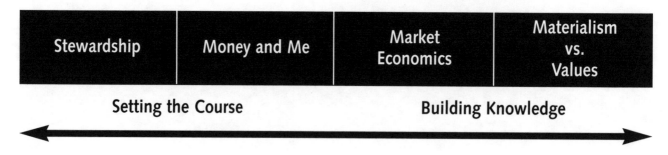

Stewardship	Money and Me	Market Economics	Materialism vs. Values

Setting the Course   Building Knowledge

Our Market-based Economy . . .

An economic system that depends on the exchange of goods and services for money.

The Market Process

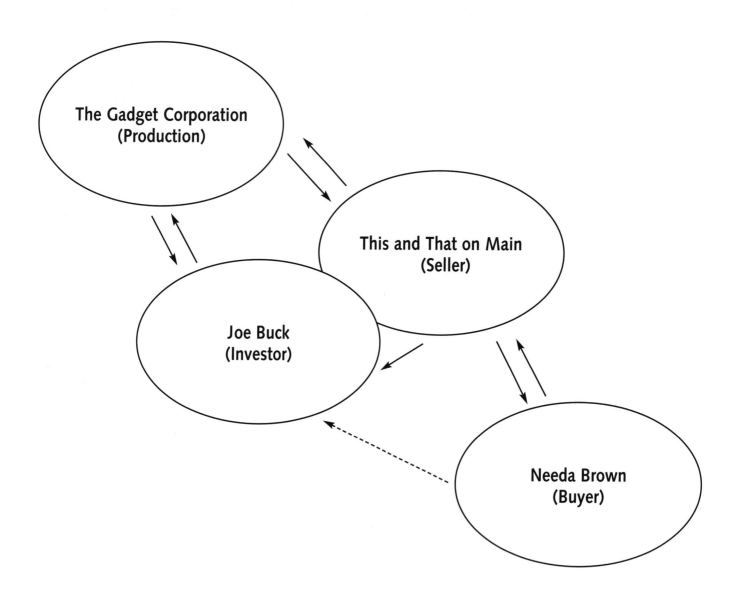

Formula for Power

ASSETS	—	LIABILITIES	=	NET WORTH
(what you own)	(minus)	(what you owe)	(equals)	(power)

Changing Behavior—Stepping Toward Financial Security

FINANCIAL SECURITY

Investing

Planning for Retirement
Stocks, Bonds, Mutual Funds

Home Ownership

Debt Management

Establishing a Good Credit History

Risk Management

Saving for Emergencies
Protecting (Insurance) Against Risks

Thrifty Living

Keys to Financial Security

To achieve financial security,

■ **live within your EARNINGS,**

■ **live below your YEARNINGS,**

■ **build on your LEARNINGS.**

Sample: What's My Risk?

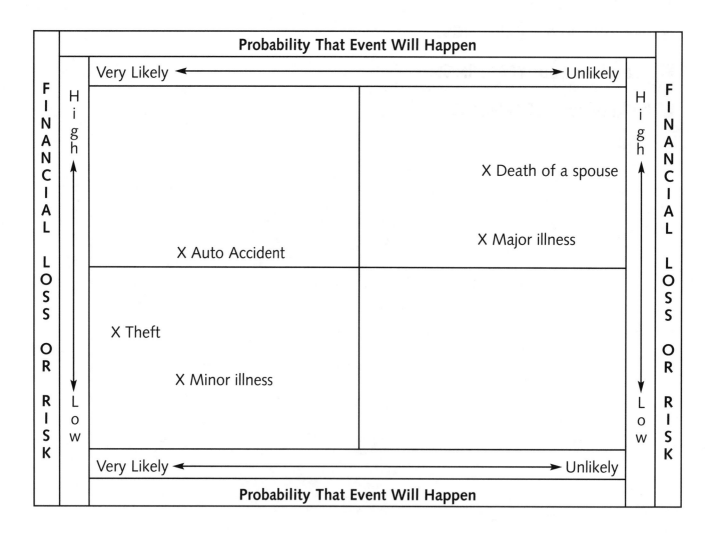

—Adapted from exercise developed by Karen Chan, University of Illinois Cooperative Extension Service, and presented at several *Faith and Finances* pilot test sites, 1999.

Dealing with Risks

■ **Avoid**

■ **Reduce**

■ **Bear**

■ **Transfer**

Types of Savings

Savings

Liquid assets that are held in the form of cash or can be readily converted to cash with minimal or no loss in value; used to meet living expenses, make purchases, pay bills and loans, and provide for emergencies and unexpected opportunities.

Types of Savings*

- **Cash**

- **Checking Account**

- **Savings Account (Passbook)**

- **Money Market Deposit Account (MMDA)**

- **Negotiable Order of Withdrawal (NOW) Account**

- **Certificate of Deposit (CD) [less than one year maturity]**

- **Money Market Mutual Fund (MMMF)**

- **U.S. Treasury bill (T-bill)**

- **U.S. Savings Bond (EE)**

*Several of these terms do not apply in the Canadian economic system.

—Excerpted from Lawrence J. Gitman and Michael D. Joehnk, *Personal Financial Planning*, 6th edition, The Dyrden Press, © 1993, pp. 53, 56, 171. Reprinted by permission of the publisher.

Four Common Types of Insurance

Automobile Insurance (PAP) [1]

Part A: Liability Coverage

Part B: Medical Payments Coverage

Part C: Uninsured Motorists Coverage

Part D: Coverage for Damage to Vehicle

■ **Collision**

■ **Comprehensive**

Property Insurance [2]

Homeowner's Insurance

■ **Renter's Insurance**

—(1) Excerpted from Lawrence J. Gitman and Michael D. Joehnk, *Personal Financial Planning*, The Dryden Press, © 1993, pp. 361, 373, 377, 379, 385, 429-431, 435, 453-459, 461-463, 465. Reprinted by permission of the publisher.

—(2) Excerpted from Author J. Keown, *Personal Finance: Turning Money into Wealth*, © 1998, Prentice-Hall, Inc., pp. 322-330. Reprinted by permission of Prentice-Hall, Inc., Upper Saddle River, NJ.

Health Insurance

Medicare [U.S.] [1]

Blue Cross/Blue Shield Plans [Canada, U.S.] [1]

Fee-for-Service or Traditional Indemnity Plan [U.S.] [2]

Managed Health Care or Prepaid Care Plan [U.S.] [2]

- Health Maintenance Organizations (HMOs)

- Individual Practice Association Plan (IPA)

- Group Practice Plan

- Point-of-Service Plan

- Preferred Provider Organization (PPO)

Life Insurance [1]

Term Life Insurance

Whole Life Insurance

Universal Life Insurance

Social Security Survivor's Benefits (U.S.)

—(1) Excerpted from Lawrence J. Gitman and Michael D. Joehnk, *Personal Financial Planning,* The Dryden Press, © 1993, pp. 361, 373, 377, 379, 385, 429-431, 435, 453-459, 461-463, 465. Reprinted by permission of the publisher.

—(2) Excerpted from Author J. Keown, *Personal Finance: Turning Money into Wealth,* © 1998, Prentice-Hall, Inc., pp. 322-330. Reprinted by permission of Prentice-Hall, Inc., Upper Saddle River, NJ.

The Cost of Home Ownership

Down Payment

Mortgage Points

Closing Costs

Mortgage Payments

- ■ **Principal**

- ■ **Interest**

- ■ **Property Taxes**

- ■ **Homeowner's Insurance**

Maintenance and Operating Expenses

Private Mortgage Insurance

—Excerpted from Lawrence J. Gitman and Michael D. Joehnk, *Personal and Financial Planning,*
The Dryden Press, © 1993, pp. 217-223. Reprinted by permission of the publisher.

Types of Investments

Assets . . . that are acquired for the purpose of earning a return rather than providing a service. [1]

Types of investments include: [2]

- **Common Stock**

- **Preferred Stock**

- **Corporate Bonds**

- **Government Bonds**

- **Muncipal Bonds**

- **Mutual Funds**

- **Employer-Sponsored Retirement Plans**

- **Individual Retirement Funds**

—(1) Excerpted from Lawrence J. Gitman and Michael D. Joehnk, *Personal Financial Planning,* The Dryden Press, © 1993, pp. 53, 495. Reprinted by permission of the publisher.

—(2) Excerpted from Arthur J. Keown, *Personal Finance: Turning Money into Wealth,* Prentice-Hall, Inc., © 1998, pp. 452, 476-481, 496, 507, 516, 520, 547, 556-560. Reprinted by permission of Prentice-Hall, Inc., Upper Saddle River, NJ.

Sources of Income for Retirement

- Earnings from Full- and Part-time Work

- Social Security (U.S.) or Old Age Security (Canada)

- Employer-sponsored Retirement Plans

- Employer-sponsored Profit-sharing Plans

- Individual Retirement Plans

- Investment Income

- Other (Welfare, Disability, Inheritance, and so on)

Long-Term Investment Performance (1926-1998)

TYPE OF INVESTMENT	RATE OF RETURN
Small Caps (small companies worth $1.3 billion or less)	12.4%
Large Caps (large companies worth $53.43 or more)	11.2%
Long-term Corporate Bonds	5.8%
Intermediate Government Bonds	5.3%
Long-term Government Bonds	5.3%
U.S. Treasury Bills	3.8%
Rate of Inflation	**3.1%**

—Data compiled and presented by Melody Hobson, Senior Vice President, Ariel Capital Management, Inc., at Wayman African Methodist Episcopal Church, Chicago, December 18, 1999.

Take $1000 . . .

INVESTED FROM 1926-1998 IN . . .	AMOUNT OF RETURN
Stocks in Small Caps	$5,080,901
Stocks Large Caps	$2,320,863
Long-term Corporate Bonds	$61,299
Intermediate Government Bonds	$43,378
Long-term Government bonds	$43,378
U.S. Treasury Bills	$15,220
Inflation Value	**$9,287**

—Data compiled and presented by Melody Hobson, Senior Vice President, Ariel Capital Management, Inc., at Wayman African Methodist Episcopal Church, Chicago, December 18, 1999.

Where Is My Money Going?

Often we spend our money for things we really don't *need* (magazines, candy, fast food, movies, cigarettes, soda pop, and so on). Even though these things may not cost a lot, the expense adds up and keeps us from saving money for real needs.

- Fill out the chart below to see how much money you might be able to save in four weeks. In the column on the left, list items you buy regularly even though you don't need them. Write down how often you buy each item in a four-week time period and the cost of the items listed. Then calculate what it costs you to buy each item over four weeks (multiply the times purchased by the price).
- Circle the items you are willing to stop buying for the next month. Calculate how much money you will save by cutting out these unnecessary items (add up the cost over four weeks for the items circled).

ITEM PURCHASED	TIMES PURCHASED IN FOUR WEEKS	COST OF ITEM	COST OVER FOUR WEEKS
Example: Magazine	4	$2.50	$10

My Total Planned Savings for One Month $ _____

My Actual Savings for One Month $ _____

My Monthly Budget

Keeping track of your monthly income and expenses will help you develop a budget. In the column on the left, you'll find a list of typical sources of income and expenses (adapt this list to meet your situation). On this page, record your monthly income from each of the sources listed. On the next two pages, record in the middle column the amount you have spent or will spend for each of these items this month. In the column on the right, estimate the amount you plan to spend for each of these items next month. This budget will help you prioritize your expenses and reach your financial goals.

DESCRIPTION	INCOME THIS MONTH
Income*	
Wages or Business Income (after taxes)	
TANF (Temporary Assistance for Needy Families)	
SSI (Supplemental Social Security)	
Food Stamps	
Pensions/Retirement/Social Security	
Child Support/Alimony	
Income from Savings and Investments	
Support from Friends and Family	
Other:	
Total Income	

*Sources of income will vary for Canadians. For example, Canada has no food stamp program but offers a Baby Bonus program that provides income to families for each child.

DESCRIPTION	ACTUAL EXPENSES THIS MONTH	PLANNED EXPENSES THIS MONTH
Expenses		
1. Stewardship/Giving Back		
Gifts		
Personal		
Charities		
Church		
2. Living Expenses		
Food		
Clothing		
Housing (rent, not mortgage payment)		
Utilities (electricity, gas, water, garbage)		
Telephone		
Child Care		
Child Support/Alimony		
Transportation (gas, auto maintenance and repair, bus or taxi fares)		
Medical Care		
3. Miscellaneous Expenses		
Recreation/Entertainment		
Other Miscellaneous Expenses		
4. Emergency Funds		
Cash kept at home		
Passbook Savings Account		
Certificates of Deposit		
Other Savings		
5. Protection Against Risks		
Auto Insurance		
Homeowners or Renters Insurance		
Health Insurance		
Life Insurance		

DESCRIPTION	ACTUAL EXPENSES THIS MONTH	PLANNED EXPENSES THIS MONTH
6. **Credit Payments**		
Credit card payments		
Auto and other consumer loans		
Real estate loan		
7. **Investments**		
Stocks		
Bonds		
Mutual Funds		
Retirement		
Other		
8. **Other Expenses**		
Total Expenses		

Monthly Balance $_____
(Total Income minus
Total Expenses)

My Financial Picture

Income/Expense

- Use your worksheet "My Monthly Budget" to complete the income and expense part of this worksheet.

  _____ Annual Income (Multiply the total monthly income from your budget worksheet by 12.)

  _____ Annual Expenses (Multiply the total monthly expenses from your budget worksheet by 12.)

  _____ Annual Balance (Subtract annual expenses from annual income.)

Assets

- List the value (what they are worth today) of any of the following assets you own. Circle those you depend on to meet annual expenses. Put a star by those you could use to reach long-term goals.

  _____ Cash

  _____ Checking accounts

  _____ Passbook savings accounts

  _____ Certificates of Deposit

  _____ Other savings

  _____ Personal property (furniture, and so on)

  _____ Real personal property (home, auto)

  _____ Stocks, bonds, mutual funds

  _____ Cash value of life insurance policies

  _____ Employer-sponsored retirement plans

  _____ Individual retirement plans

  _____ Business real estate (apartment building, office or industrial site, other)

  _____ Sole-owner business or limited partnerships

  _____ Other assets

  _____ Total Value of Assets

Snapshot

- My financial "picture" looks (check one)

  _____ focused (I'm managing my money well).

  _____ fuzzy (I'm not completely in control of my money.)

  _____ out of focus (I don't have clear goals for managing my money.)

My Financial Goals

In his heart a man plans his course, but the LORD determines his steps.
—Proverbs 16:9

The Goal-Setting Process

Step 1
Write down the one long-term financial goal most important to you right now. (A long-term goal is something you can accomplish in one to four years.)

Step 2
Write down one short-term goal that will help you reach the long-term goal you described in Step 1. (A short-term goal is one that you can do in the next six months.)

Step 3
Identify what you will need to reach your long-term goal.

Time _____

Money_____

Other resources (list the kinds of information you need, people who can help you, skills you have or need to develop, and so on) _____

_____

_____

Step 4
Write down a plan (who, what, when, where, how) for reaching this long-term goal.

Step 5

Evaluate your plan. Share your goal with others in the group and discuss these questions with them (or with your mentor):

- What are the pros and cons of your plan?
- What things might get in the way?
- What will help you succeed at this when others might fail?
- Are you still determined to reach this goal?

Setting Financial Goals

My Short-term Goals

SHORT-TERM GOAL (I WANT, I WILL, I NEED . . .)	TIME NEEDED	TOTAL COST	AMOUNT TO SAVE EACH MONTH/WEEK	PLAN TO REACH MY GOAL
Example: I need to buy my son a suit for the school dance.	2 months	$100	$12.50 a week	Bring lunch to work and cut back on soda and snacks.

My Long-term Goals

LONG-TERM GOAL	TIME NEEDED	TOTAL COST	AMOUNT TO SAVE EACH MONTH/WEEK	PLAN TO REACH MY GOAL
Example: I want to buy my own home.	4 years	$4000	$50-75 a month	Join IDA program, and use tips from *Faith and Finance* program

The Language of Our Market Economy

Match these words to the correct definitions by writing the corresponding letter in the blanks on the left.

a. Assets
b. Market
c. Liability (debt)
d. Depreciation
e. Appreciation
f. Wealth
g. Home
h. Car
i. Market-based economy
j. Income
k. Inflation
l. Net worth

_____ 1. A place where goods and services are sold.

_____ 2. Something you owe and must repay.

_____ 3. An increase in the value of something.

_____ 4. An example of something that increases in value.

_____ 5. Received for work, as gifts, from social welfare, or from investments.

_____ 6. An economic system based on the exchange of goods and services for money.

_____ 7. The result after subtracting liabilities from assets.

_____ 8. The total financial resources a person accumulates over a lifetime.

_____ 9. A decrease in the value of something.

_____ 10. An example of something that decreases in value.

_____ 11. A reduction in the value of money; the dollar is worth less as prices go up.

_____ 12. Possessions that can cover one's liabilities.

Market Process Role Play Cards

Speaker #1: Joe Buck (Investor)

Hello. *(Shake hands and direct your remarks to the producer, the corporate CEO.)* I'm Joe Buck, and I'm ready to invest in your company. I've heard that you're doing well with your latest gadget and I'd like to get in on this market.

Speaker #2: The Gadget Corporation CEO (Producer)

Well, Mr. Buck, I'm glad to hear that. This new gadget *(hold the gadget in your hand, admiring it as you speak)* certainly looks promising. Let's set you up for an appointment with our investment department—it's investors like you that keep our corporation going. Then I'll have to run—got an important meeting with a big retailer on Main Street. *(Walk away, fiddle with the gadget, and pause briefly before greeting the seller.)*

It's good to see you again! My, your business is really booming—looks like you've got about every gadget around—except this one. I'd sure like to see this on display here.

Speaker #3: Owner of This and That on Main Street (Seller)

Well, let me have a look at this gadget. *(Inspect the gadget carefully.)* I must say you really come up with some nifty ideas—but I'm just not sure my customers would go wild for this. And I thought the wholesale price in your catalog was a bit steep. Tell you what—I'll take a dozen to try them out. If they sell well, then you've got a deal! *(Shake hands with producer; producer leaves gadget with seller.)*

Speaker #4: Needa Brown (Buyer)

(Greet seller as you "shop" the shelves, hunting for a gadget.) This is the neatest store—more gadgets than I knew I could buy. I really need a . . . *(describe a feature of the gadget the producer gave to the seller).* Oh! Here's just the gadget I've been looking for—and the price isn't bad. I'll take two—might come in handy for a gift.

(If you prefer, make a different consumer decision. Look at the gadget, find something not quite to your liking about it, and leave the store without purchasing it.)

Consumer Caution Card

Consumer Caution Card

When you're tempted to buy something and not sure if you should, ask yourself these questions:

- Am I buying this to make my body look better?
- Am I buying this to get back at someone?
- Am I buying this to make myself feel better?
- Am I buying this to "belong" or fit in?
- Am I buying this to impress someone?
- Do I *need* this, or do I just *want* it?
- Can I live without this?
- Have I budgeted for this?
- Am I going to regret buying this tomorrow?

Just say "no!" Put your wallet back in your pocket or purse and walk away!

—Adapted from *All My Money*, University of Illinois Cooperative Extension Service, 1997.

Consumer Caution Card

When you're tempted to buy something and not sure if you should, ask yourself these questions:

- Am I buying this to make my body look better?
- Am I buying this to get back at someone?
- Am I buying this to make myself feel better?
- Am I buying this to "belong" or fit in?
- Am I buying this to impress someone?
- Do I *need* this, or do I just *want* it?
- Can I live without this?
- Have I budgeted for this?
- Am I going to regret buying this tomorrow?

Just say "no!" Put your wallet back in your pocket or purse and walk away!

—Adapted from *All My Money*, University of Illinois Cooperative Extension Service, 1997.

Consumer Caution Card

When you're tempted to buy something and not sure if you should, ask yourself these questions:

- Am I buying this to make my body look better?
- Am I buying this to get back at someone?
- Am I buying this to make myself feel better?
- Am I buying this to "belong" or fit in?
- Am I buying this to impress someone?
- Do I *need* this, or do I just *want* it?
- Can I live without this?
- Have I budgeted for this?
- Am I going to regret buying this tomorrow?

Just say "no!" Put your wallet back in your pocket or purse and walk away!

—Adapted from *All My Money*, University of Illinois Cooperative Extension Service, 1997.

Consumer Caution Card

When you're tempted to buy something and not sure if you should, ask yourself these questions:

- Am I buying this to make my body look better?
- Am I buying this to get back at someone?
- Am I buying this to make myself feel better?
- Am I buying this to "belong" or fit in?
- Am I buying this to impress someone?
- Do I *need* this, or do I just *want* it?
- Can I live without this?
- Have I budgeted for this?
- Am I going to regret buying this tomorrow?

Just say "no!" Put your wallet back in your pocket or purse and walk away!

—Adapted from *All My Money*, University of Illinois Cooperative Extension Service, 1997.

Consumer Caution Card

When you're tempted to buy something and not sure if you should, ask yourself these questions:

- Am I buying this to make my body look better?
- Am I buying this to get back at someone?
- Am I buying this to make myself feel better?
- Am I buying this to "belong" or fit in?
- Am I buying this to impress someone?
- Do I *need* this, or do I just *want* it?
- Can I live without this?
- Have I budgeted for this?
- Am I going to regret buying this tomorrow?

Just say "no!" Put your wallet back in your pocket or purse and walk away!

—Adapted from *All My Money*, University of Illinois Cooperative Extension Service, 1997.

Consumer Caution Card

When you're tempted to buy something and not sure if you should, ask yourself these questions:

- Am I buying this to make my body look better?
- Am I buying this to get back at someone?
- Am I buying this to make myself feel better?
- Am I buying this to "belong" or fit in?
- Am I buying this to impress someone?
- Do I *need* this, or do I just *want* it?
- Can I live without this?
- Have I budgeted for this?
- Am I going to regret buying this tomorrow?

Just say "no!" Put your wallet back in your pocket or purse and walk away!

—Adapted from *All My Money*, University of Illinois Cooperative Extension Service, 1997.

These Values Are . . . to Me

Values are what you treasure or rate highly. They influence your goals, decisions, and actions.

- The column on the left lists values treasured by our society. Add other values to the list that influence you.
- Rate each value by putting an X in the column that most closely describes how important each value is to you.

VALUE	UNIMPORTANT	SOMEWHAT IMPORTANT	VERY IMPORTANT
Achievement			
Family			
Financial security			
Friends			
Fun, pleasure			
Health			
Independence			
Integrity			
Self-indulgence			
Self-worth, self-esteem			
Service to others			
Simple lifestyle			
Social justice			
Social status			
Spirituality			
Other:			
Other:			
Other:			

—Adapted from Karen Chan and others, *All My Money*, University of Illinois Cooperative Extension Service, 1997.

Values and $$

Match these values to the behaviors by writing the corresponding letter in the blanks on the left.

a. **Achievement**
b. **Family**
c. **Financial security**
d. **Friends**
e. **Fun, pleasure**
f. **Health**
g. **Independence**
h. **Integrity**
i. **Self-indulgence**
j. **Self-worth, self-esteem**
k. **Service to others**
l. **Simple lifestyle**
m. **Social justice**
n. **Social status**
o. **Spirituality**

_____ 1. Sue only spends money on the necessities.

_____ 2. Claudie has a closet full of the latest fashions yet just can't resist a sale.

_____ 3. Mabel buys organic foods because she thinks they are better for her body.

_____ 4. Jorge would rather spend money for golfing than save for his retirement.

_____ 5. Jenetta sends money to a missionary family and prays for them every week.

_____ 6. Dora pays high rent so that she can live alone.

_____ 7. Martha refuses to buy products made in sweatshops by child workers.

_____ 8. Sung buys makeup so when she looks in the mirror she feels better about herself.

_____ 9. Jed gives money to the homeless shelter and volunteers there once a month.

_____ 10. Jake, a banker, never tells anyone that he grew up in a slum neighborhood.

_____ 11. Hattie worries if she doesn't have any money in savings for emergencies.

_____ 12. John and Katie have remodeled their home so John's mother can live with them.

_____ 13. Rodney would rather spend time with his friends than work extra hours.

_____ 14. Samantha studies very hard so that she can get into medical school.

_____ 15. Hosea is disgusted that his brother doesn't repay him for a loan as promised.

What's My Power Worth?

Calculate your power (net worth) by completing the chart below.

- List the value of your assets (what they're worth today) in the blank column on the left (see the worksheet "My Financial Picture" for these numbers).
- List the amount of any liabilities (loans) you owe against these assets in the middle column.
- Subtract your liabilities from assets to determine the net worth of each asset, and record these numbers in the blank column on the right.
- Add the numbers in the right-hand column to determine your total net worth.

ASSETS	ASSETS VALUE	AMOUNT OWED	NET WORTH
Cash			
Checking accounts			
Passbook savings accounts			
Certificates of Deposit			
Other savings			
Personal property (furniture, and so on)			
Real personal property (home, auto)			
Stocks, bonds, mutual funds			
Cash value of life insurance policies			
Employer-sponsored retirement plans			
Individual retirement plans			
Business real estate (apartment building, office or industrial site, other)			
Sole-owner business or limited partnerships			
Other Assets			
Total Net Worth			

Review your financial picture again and think about these questions:

- Will your net worth provide financial security right now? in the future?
- What short-term goals can you meet with your present net worth? (Refer back to the worksheet "My Financial Goals.")
- What changes will you need to make to build your net worth (power) in order to meet your long-term goals (see "My Financial Goals" worksheet)?
- Where can you start? Who can help you? What other resources do you need? (Check your list on the "My Financial Goals" worksheet, and add any new people and other resources you've identified.)

Do I Really Need This—Or Do I Just Want It?

Complete this chart as part of your plan for thrifty living.

- In the column on the left, list five items that you are thinking about purchasing in the next month.
- Estimate the cost of each item. (Use catalogs, store fliers, and advertisements to figure the cost.)
- Indicate if this item is a *want* or a *need.*
- Then rank how important purchasing this item is to you. (1 means that you urgently need this item, 2 means that it would be helpful to have this item soon, and 3 means that you could live without it at least for now.)
- In the column on the right, describe ways that you could be more thrifty when purchasing this item.

ITEM	COST	WANT OR NEED?	IMPORTANCE OF PURCHASE (rate from 1 to 3)	WAYS TO BE MORE THRIFTY
Example: Nike running shoes	$100	Want	3	Buy a cheaper brand. Wait for sales.

—Adapted from Karen Chan and others, *All My Money,* University of Illinois Cooperative Extension Service, 1997.

Thrifty Tips

You can be thrifty by saving small amounts of money. Before long the dollars you save can add up to larger amounts. For example, if you make your own coffee rather than buying a cup of flavored coffee several times each week, you could save over $300 in one year! Try some of these other thrifty tips, and watch your savings grow!

Food

$ Make a shopping list and stick to it! Only use coupons for products you normally buy.

$ Don't pay extra for the packaging. Avoid products that are individually wrapped.

$ Buy store-brand or generic brand items.

$ Bring your lunch and snacks to work.

$ Cut down on eating out. Have a potluck with friends or make the same dishes at home.

$ Comparison shop. Calculate the cost per unit of weight (ounces, pounds, liters/quarts).

$ Find local programs (for example, neighborhood co-ops) or wholesalers that sell food for less.

Clothing

$ Buy clothes at thrift shops or consignment shops, especially for children who grow quickly.

$ Watch for end-of-season sales, but don't buy something just because it's on sale.

$ Buy clothes that will stay in fashion longer; avoid the latest trend that will go out of style in one season.

$ Have clothing swaps with friends and family.

$ Buy washable fabrics to save on dry cleaning costs.

Utilities

$ In the winter, turn the thermostat down and wear warmer clothes around the house.

$ In the summer, use fans instead of an air conditioner.

$ Turn off lights—and the television—when leaving a room.

$ Write letters instead of making long distance calls.

$ Make long distance calls when rates are cheapest.

$ Dry clothes outside or on a rack.

$ Defrost the refrigerator or freezer when the frost is about 1/4 inch thick.

Entertainment

$ Walk, run, join a community sports team. (Exercising helps you stay healthy and avoid medical bills.)

$ Borrow books, magazines, CDs, cassettes, and videotapes from the library.

$ Plan family or neighborhood picnics.

$ Purchase games, puzzles, and so on at garage sales, and plan a family fun night.

$ Go to matinee movies. Buy tickets to theater shows the day of the event.

$ Buy used bikes, wagons, and other toys at garage sales.

Other Tips

$ Cut your children's hair.

$ Wash your car and change the oil yourself.

$ Carpool to work or take public transportation.

—Adapted from a *Faith and Finances* pilot test presentation at Wayman African Methodist Episcopal Church, Chicago, by Rhonda Hardy, Consumer and Family Economics Educator, University of Illinois Cooperative Extension Service, August 14, 1999.

Request for Credit Report*

Personal Data

Name: _____
      (last)   (middle)   (first)

Birthdate: _____

Social Security Number: _____

Home Address: _____
              (street)   (city)   (state)   (zip)

Address Verification

If you have moved in the past six months, enclose *copies* of two of the items listed below (check which two you are enclosing):

_____ driver's license or state ID card

_____ utility bill mailed to current address

_____ phone bill mailed to current address

_____ bank statement mailed to current address

List other addresses where you have lived in the past five years (if applicable):

Other Information

Spouse's name (if applicable):_____

Other names used to apply for credit (if applicable): _____

Credit Status (Check all that apply and enclose the requested information.)

_____ I have been denied credit, employment, or insurance in the past 60 days. (Enclose a copy of the letter of refusal.) Please send me a free report.

_____ I am currently receiving Temporary Assistance to Needy Families (TANF). (Enclose a copy of a check stub or medical ID card.) Please send me a free report.

_____ I do not qualify for a free report. (Enclose a check or money order for the correct amount—see phone number of credit bureau to check the amount required.)

Signature: _____

Date: _____

Mail this report request to one of these credit bureaus:

Trans Union
P.O. Box 390
Springfield, PA 19064-0390
1-800-916-8800
(You will be referred to your
area credit agency.)

Experian
P.O. Box 2104
Allen, TX 75013-2104
1-800-682-7654

Equifax
P.O. Box 105873
Atlanta, GA 30348
1-800-685-1111

*This form is applicable to U.S. citizens. Process in Canada may vary; credit bureau information will be different.

What's My Risk?

Life is full of unexpected events, some which change our lives forever. Complete this worksheet to assess how some events could affect your life.

- On the back of this worksheet, list all the events that might occur in your life that could affect your financial security.
- Then determine how likely each event is apt to occur and what the degree of financial loss (risk) might be.
- Write the event in the spot in one of the four boxes that best marks the probability and financial loss of this event. (We've provided one example for you, describing the impact death of a spouse might have on a family.)

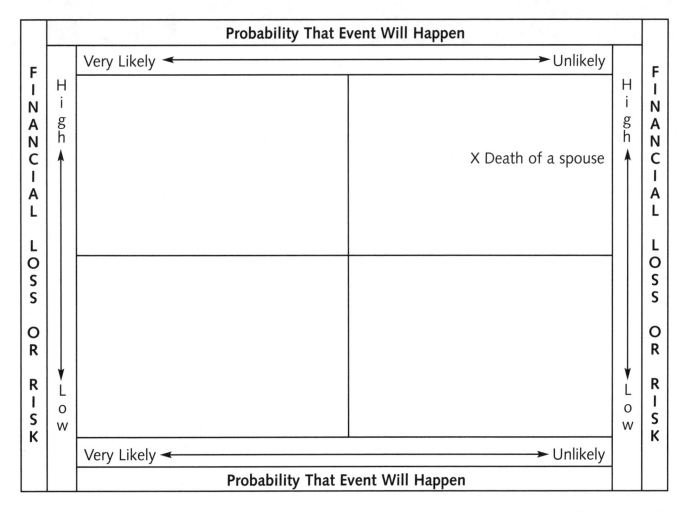

—Adapted from exercise developed by Karen Chan, University of Illinois Cooperative Extension Service, and presented at several *Faith and Finances* pilot test sites.

My Protection Plan

You've already identified what risks or losses you would like to transfer to insurance companies. Now you're ready to develop a plan for managing those risks.

- On the back of this worksheet, list the events you circled and didn't star on the worksheet "What's My Risk?" (These are the risks or losses you wish to transfer to insurance companies.)
- Number these events in the order of priority. Number one should be the event that you think is most urgently in need of insurance protection.
- Complete the chart below to describe what insurance will meet your needs for protection for the event you listed as number one. (If possible, you'll want to do some comparison shopping.)

EVENT (Priority #1)	COMPANY (Name, address, phone #)	TYPE OF COVERAGE (Major Protection Features)	DEDUCTIBLES ($ amount per year or event)	MONTHLY PREMIUM ($ amount)

Shopping Notes
What did you learn that made you choose this policy?

Budget Adjustments
Where will you find the money in your budget needed to pay the premium for this coverage?

(If you are ready to purchase additional insurance protection, repeat this exercise for each type of insurance coverage needed.)

My Credit History

Use your credit report to complete this exercise. (If you haven't received your report yet, fill in as much of the worksheet as you can and complete it when the report arrives.)

My Credit Rating

What words are used on your credit report to describe your current credit history? (For example, if your history with a particular creditor is good, the report may say, "Open, never late.") Write these words below and note how often each different phrase is used on your report.

Causes (Events)

If your credit rating is poor, what events may have contributed to your current credit history? Check all those below that apply to your situation.

_____ Medical crisis

_____ Loss of job

_____ Decrease in wages or business income

_____ Separation or divorce

_____ Death of spouse

_____ Gambling

_____ Overspending

_____ Other (explain):

Bills Coming Due

Whether or not your credit history is bad, complete the chart on the back of this handout.

- List all bills that are coming due in the next two months.
- Star any creditors who gave you a poor rating on your credit report.
- Answer the questions below the chart.

I Owe . . .

CREDITOR	FOR . . .	DATE DUE	AMOUNT DUE	INTEREST RATE	AMOUNT PLANNING TO PAY	DATE PAID

- What bill has the highest interest rate? Should you be paying off this bill first? If so, how can you pay off this bill faster without missing other payments?

- What bills can you pay off in the next several months? How will you do this?

- Can you reduce bills for utilities, transportation, or other items in the next several months? How?

- What else can you do in the next several months to improve your credit history?

More About Credit

If you want to know about credit and how to improve your credit rating, contact any of these agencies:

Consumer Credit Counseling Services (CCCS)
24-hour phone line: 800-388-2227
Spanish phone line: 800-682-9832
Website: www.nfcc.org

These offices, under the umbrella of the National Foundation for Credit Counseling, provide tips on credit management and individual credit counseling. Call the toll-free numbers or check the Website to find the Neighborhood Financial Care Center nearest you. Visit your area office or call 800-669-2635 for a free copy of *Coping with a Credit Crisis*.

Federal Reserve Bank
Website: www.federalreserve.gov/otherfrb.htm

Visit the Website for a listing of the various Federal Reserve districts or check the government listings in your phone book. Request free brochures on credit and debt repair.

Federal Trade Commission
Phone: 202-326-2421
Website: www.ftc/gov

Request *Facts for Consumers*, a series of free pamphlets related to credit, or *Building a Better Credit Record*, a free booklet that explains credit history, credit reports, and how to deal with credit problems.

MyVesta.org
Phone: 800-680-3328
Website: myvesta.org

Formerly the Debt Counselors of America, MyVesta.org is an Internet-based nonprofit agency providing debt counseling, financial recovery counseling, online bill management, and other services. Numerous self-help resources are available.

The National Center for Financial Education
Website: www.ncfe.org

To order *The Do-It-Yourself Credit File Correction Guide*, send $12 to NCFE, P.O Box WWW-34070, San Diego, CA 92163.

Why I Want to Own a Home

There are many reasons for wanting to own a home. Check all those below that best describe why you want to own a home.

Emotional Benefits

Home ownership would give my family

_____ a sense of stability.

_____ a place to be together.

_____ self-respect and pride.

_____ a feeling of belonging and connection.

_____ security and peace of mind.

_____ other emotional reasons (describe):

Financial Benefits

Home ownership would give my family more financial security because

_____ a home is a tangible asset (one that I can touch and see).

_____ a home may appreciate in value over time and protect against inflation.

_____ the interest and property taxes can be deducted from my income tax (if I itemize deductions).

_____ in case of emergency, I can borrow against the equity (the difference between what the home is worth and what I owe).

_____ I can contribute "sweat equity" by doing some remodeling or maintenance (painting, redecorating, landscaping, and so on) to increase the resale value.

_____ other financial reasons (describe):

—Adapted from *Faith and Finances* Cabrini pilot test presentation by Ruth Wuorenma, president, Neighborhood Capital Company LLC, November, 1999.

Am I Ready to Buy a Home?

Buying a home is a big step. You will need to consider the cost to obtain a loan and the long-term costs of paying for and maintaining your home. Are you ready to take this step? To help you decide, answer these questions:

- Give yourself 5 points for each "Yes" answer.
- Give yourself -10 points for each "No" answer.
- Add up the points and use the key at the bottom of the page to determine your readiness.
- Answer the questions about your score.

YES	NO	QUESTION	POINTS
		Have you done the same type of work for at least two years?	
		Will you have a stable and adequate income for the next five years?	
		Have you had a good credit rating for at least one year? (You can establish credit by paying your utility bills on time each month.)	
		Do you have savings to pay for the down payment and closing costs? (Typically you will need to put down at least 3-5 percent of the purchase price plus closing costs.)	
		Do you keep good records (tax returns, credit reports, income and expense records, and so on)?	
		Are you able to pay for the maintenance and operation (utility) costs of a home?	
		Are interest rates reasonable for home mortgages?	
		Total Score _____	

Key:
If your score is

+5 and above: Consider buying a home.
-5 to +5: Think twice about buying a home. Consider waiting.
-5 and below: Wait to buy a home.

- Is this about how ready to buy a home you thought you would be? Why or why not?
- What's your next step?

—Adapted from *Faith and Finances* Bronzeville pilot test presentation by Alex Carlucci, Senior Loan Officer, Prism Mortgage Company, February 2000.

Am I Preparing for Retirement?

Preparing for retirement is a long-term goal. Financial security in your retirement years will depend on the time you have to prepare, your sources of retirement income, and the steps you to take to manage your retirement income.

Time

How many years do you have left to prepare?

- Age you're planning to retire _____
- minus your age now _____
- equals the number of years you have to prepare _____.

Income

What sources of income do you plan to use for retirement? (Place an X in one of the columns to the right that best describes each source of retirement income listed on the left.)

SOURCES OF INCOME	DEPENDABLE SOURCE	POSSIBLE SOURCE	UNLIKELY SOURCE	NEED TO CONSIDER THIS SOURCE
Earnings from Full- or Part-time Work*				
Social Security (U.S.) or Old Age Security (Can.)				
Employer-sponsored Retirement Plans				
Employer-sponsored Profit-sharing Plans				
Individual Retirement Plans				
Investment Income				
Other (describe):				

*In the U.S., the earnings cap for social security recipients ages 65 through 69 was removed in 2000, allowing them unlimited earnings while still receiving Social Security benefits.

Steps

Considering the number of years you have left to prepare for retirement and the sources of income you've checked, how prepared are you for retirement?

_____ Well prepared

_____ Somewhat prepared

_____ Unprepared

If you're not well prepared, here are some steps you can take now to plan for retirement:

Step 1. Learn more about Social Security (U.S.) or Old Age Security (Canada).

Step 2. Learn about your employer's retirement or profit-sharing plans.

Step 3. Contribute to a tax-sheltered savings plan [401(k), 403(b), annuities].

Step 4. Contribute to an individual retirement plan [Keogh, IRAs, Roth IRAs (U.S.) or RRSPs (Canada)].

Step 5. Invest in stocks, bonds, and mutual funds.

What's *your* next step? Describe what you will do and what information you will need.

How Much Risk Can I Take?

Generally, the higher the rate of return on an investment, the higher the risk. How much risk are you willing to take to build financial security and to build wealth to meet long-term goals? Look at the diagram below and circle what savings and investments seem best for you.

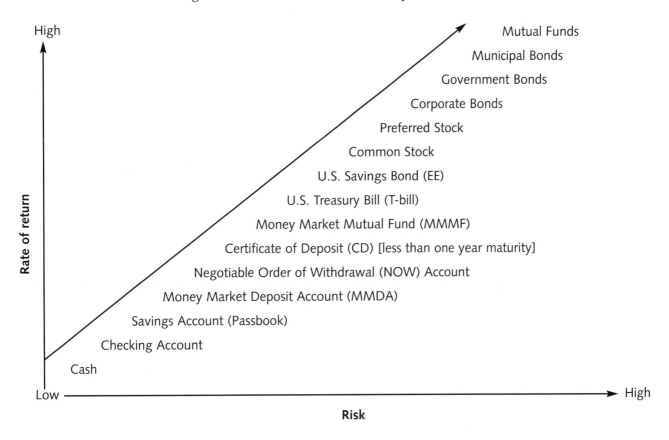

Rule of Thumb
- When money is needed within one year, it should be *saved* in checking or savings accounts, money market deposit accounts, or certificates of deposit.
- When money is needed within five years, at least 50 percent should be *saved* in a money market mutual fund or government bonds/bill/notes or *invested* in municipal or corporate bond funds.
- When money isn't needed within ten years or more, a larger percentage can be *invested* in stocks.

What's Important to Me?

When we invest in a company, our values and goals influence our decisions. Below we've listed several issues that may affect your decision to invest in a particular company. (We've identified if an issue has a social or financial impact.)

Rank each issue using this scale:

1 - Very Important
2 - Important
3 - Unimportant

When investing, I . . .

_____ consider the diversity of the board of directors (social).

_____ prefer to have someone else (a broker or financial planner) make my investment decisions (financial).

_____ consider whether the corporation makes guns (social).

_____ want to earn the greatest return possible (financial).

_____ am concerned about the corporation's environmental impact (social).

_____ want to be sure that my investment is not supporting an oppressive government (social).

_____ invest in companies who think about long-term value more than immediate profits (financial).

_____ oppose the use of overseas sweatshop labor (social).

_____ insist that some of the money is invested in my own community (social).

- Are social issues more important to you than financial issues when you choose a company for your investment dollars?
- Are your financial and social values sometimes in conflict?

Appendix

Language as Ministry

Savings Options

Insurance—Protection Against Risks

The Cost of Home Ownership

Some Investment Options

Optional Session Plan:
Investment Clubs

Language as Ministry

Many of the activities, from reading handouts to filling out worksheets, in this *Faith and Finances* program require reading skills. You'll want to be sure that participants who read very little or not at all do not feel left out of some aspects of group work or cut off from individual opportunities to learn more about managing their money.

How To Tell If a Participant Can't Read (1)

(The following clues to a participant's possible illiteracy were adapted for this program from clues developed by Cathy Roth, tutor-student coordinator of the Literacy Volunteers of America Lancaster-Lebanon Literacy Council in Pennsylvania.)

Observe if a participant

- takes "simple" forms or worksheets home to fill out.
- supplies large quantities of information over the phone rather than through the mail.
- makes an excuse for not reading along during group activities (for example, "I forgot my glasses," or "I have a headache").
- doesn't move eyes over the page when reading silently.
- never responds to personalized mail.
- "forgets" appointments or events he or she seems interested in.
- turns down opportunities requiring reading and writing (for example, contacting a bank for information or sending for a credit history).
- doesn't use the handouts to complete activities.
- talks about his or her children's trouble in school.
- makes donations or pays for supplies in cash.

Some Recommended Bible Translations (2)

When choosing Scripture versions to use, consider the reading level of Bible versions or translations. Here are some recommended ones:

- *New International Reader's Version* (2.9 grade level)
  Zondervan Publishing House (800-727-3480)

  This version is an excellent simplification of the *New International Version,* the most widely used English Bible. The NIrV is a very readable version for both adults and children. It contains many special features and helps to aid understanding.

- *GOD'S WORD* (4th-5th grade level)
  God's Word to the Nations Bible Society (877-463-7967)

  This version is outstanding for its accurate and readable translation.

- *New Century Version* (3rd and 5th grade level)
  Word, Inc. (800-933-9673)

Adapted from a translation for the deaf, the NCV began as the *International Children's Bible* and later became the *Everyday Bible* (now out of print, both at 3rd grade level). The standard NCV is now written at 5th grade level.

- *Contemporary English Version* (5th grade level)
American Bible Society (800-322-4253)

The CEV Project was begun in 1984 by the American Bible Society. Both the adult version and illustrated children's version have many reading aids.

- *New Living Translation* (6.4 grade level)
Tyndale House Publishers (800-323-9400)

The NLT is largely a replacement for the very popular *Living Bible*, although the *Living Bible* will continue to be published.

- *Easy-to-Read Version* (4th grade level)
World Bible Translation Center, Inc. (817-595-1664)

This version was especially prepared to meet the needs of the deaf, those learning English as a second language, and those facing special reading difficulties. It served as the basis for the *New Century Version* and the *International Children's Bible*.

- *New Life Version* (3rd grade level)
Christian Literature International (800-324-9734)

This version is based on a vocabulary of about 850 words. It was translated by missionary Gleason H. Ledyard. Because of the limited number of words, some verses aren't expressed quite as clearly.

Ministry Resources

If you are interested in information about starting a language ministry in your church or organization, contact

CRC (Christian Reformed Church) Publications
OPEN DOOR MINISTRIES
2850 Kalamazoo Ave. SE
Grand Rapids, MI 49560
Phone: 616-246-0753 or 800-333-8300
Website: www.crcpublications.org

Ruth Vander Hart, Editor, OPEN DOOR BOOKS
E-mail: vanderhr@crcpublications.org

Alice Berry, Program Developer, OPEN DOOR BOOKS
E-mail: aliceb@allegan.net

Gail Rice, Literacy Consultant, OPEN DOOR BOOKS
E-mail: Gailvrice@aol.com

—(1) Adapted from *Opening Minds, Changing Lives*, Program Packet, Open Door Ministries (CRC Publications), pp. 4-5.

—(2) Abstracted from Gail Rice, *Easy-Reading Scripture Versions*, © 1999, Gail Rice, p. 1. Used by permission of Gail Rice.

Savings Options

Savings are *liquid assets* that are held in the form of cash or can be readily converted to cash with minimal or no loss in value, used to meet living expenses, make purchases, pay bills and loans, and provide for emergencies and unexpected opportunities.

Types of savings include

- **Cash.** Pocket money—the coins and currency in one's possession.

- **Checking Accounts.** A *demand deposit,* meaning that the withdrawal of these funds must be permitted whenever demanded by the account holder. Regular checking . . . pays no interest . . . [and] can be offered only by commercial banks.

- **Savings Accounts.** A *passbook account*—a savings account in which transactions are sometimes recorded in a passbook—pays the going passbook rate of interest.

- **Money Market Deposit Accounts (MMDA).** A savings account that is meant to be competitive with a MMMF [Money Market Mutual Fund], offered by banks and other depository institutions.

- **Negotiable Order of Withdrawal (NOW) Accounts.** A checking account on which the financial institution can pay whatever rate of interest it deems appropriate.

  MMDAs and Now accounts . . . are available at virtually every deposit-taking financial institution . . . and are marketed under various names (Checkomatic Accounts, Prime Checking, Preferred Checking, Premium Accounts, and so on). Most require maintaining a minimum balance to earn interest; some limit the number of withdrawals per month.

- **Certificate of Deposit (CD).** A savings instrument where funds are left on deposit for a stipulated period of time (one week to one year or more); imposes a penalty for withdrawing funds early. Market yields [interest rates] vary by size and maturity; no check-writing privileges.

- **Money Market Mutual Fund (MMMF).** A mutual fund that pools the funds of many small investors and purchases high-yielding, short-term marketable securities offered by the U.S. Treasury, major corporations, large commercial banks, and various government organizations. MMMFs generally pay interest at rates considerably above (2 to 5 percent) those paid on regular savings accounts. . . . Investors have instant access to their funds through check-writing privileges, although checks often must be written for a stipulated minimum amount (usually $500).

Deposit insurance protects funds on deposit against failure of the institution [commercial banks, savings and loans, credit unions]. Insuring agencies include the *Federal Deposit Insurance Corporation (FDIC)* and the *National*

Credit Union Administration (NCUA). [This applies to all types of savings accounts described above except money market mutual funds.]

- **U.S. Treasury Bill (T-bill).** Short-term, highly marketable security issued by the U.S. Treasury (originally issued with maturities of 13, 26, and 62 weeks); smallest denomination is $10,000.

- **U.S. Savings Bond (EE).** Issued by U.S. Treasury; rate of interest is tied to U.S. Treasury securities. Long a popular savings vehicle (widely used with payroll deduction plans). Maturities are approximately five years; sold in denominations of $500 or more.

—Excerpted from Lawrence J. Gitman and Michael D. Joehnk,
Personal Financial Planning, The Dryden Press, © 1993,
pp. 174-177. Reprinted by permission of the publisher.

Insurance—Protection Against Risks

Automobile Insurance (1)

[The] Personal Auto Policy (PAP) [is] a comprehensive automobile insurance policy . . . easily understood by the "typical" insurance purchaser. . . . The coverages provided in the policy . . . are as follows:

- Part A: Liability coverage
Protects individuals against losses from bodily injury; . . . [and] covers damage to property on a per-accident basis. . . . The insurer agrees to settle or defend any claim or suit asking for such damages.

- Part B: Medical payments coverage
Provides for payment to a covered person of an amount no greater than the policy limits for all reasonable and necessary medical expenses incurred within three years of an automobile accident.

- Part C: Uninsured motorists coverage
[Protects] . . . innocent accident victims who are involved in an accident in which an uninsured or underinsured motorist is at fault.

- Part D: Coverage for damage to your vehicle
Collision insurance . . . pays for collision damage to an insured automobile regardless of who was at fault.

  Comprehensive automobile insurance . . . provides protection against loss to an insured automobile caused by any peril other than collision.

You are almost sure to purchase liability, medical payments, and uninsured motorists protection. You may, however, choose *not* to buy protection against damage to your automobile if it is "worn" and of relatively little value. . . . If you have a loan against your car, you will probably be *required* to have the physical damage coverage—part D—at least equal to the amount of the loan.

Property Insurance (1)

Homeowner's Insurance

Four different forms (HO-1, HO-2, HO-3, and HO-8) are . . . available to homeowners, and two other forms (HO-4 and HO-6) are designed to meet the needs of renters and owners of condominiums. . . . All HO (Homeowner's) forms are divided into two sections.

- Section I applies to the dwelling, its contents, and accompanying structures.
- Section II deals with comprehensive coverage for personal liability and for medical payments to others.

The forms differ in that the scope of coverage under Section I is least with an HO-1 policy and greatest with an HO-3 policy. HO-8 is a modified coverage policy for older homes . . . that have market values well below their costs to rebuild. The coverage in Section II is the same for all forms.

The homeowner's coverage on a house and the accompanying structures is [often] based on *replacement cost coverage* (the amount necessary to repair, rebuild, or replace an asset at today's prices). . . . In order to be eligible for reimbursement on a replacement-cost basis, a homeowner must keep the home insured for at least 80 percent of the amount it would cost to build it today exclusive of the value of the land. . . . For a nominal cost, homeowners can purchase an *inflaction protection rider*, whereby the amount of coverage is automatically adjusted for the effects of inflation.

Standard coverage on the contents may be on an *actual cash value basis*. Therefore, depreciation is taken into account in calculating the amount of any payments made for losses of furniture, clothing, and other belongings.

Renter's Insurance

A standard renter's policy [Form HO-4] covers furniture, carpets, appliances, clothing, and most other personal items for their cash value at the time of the loss. For maximum protection, you can buy replacement cost insurance. . . . The HO-4 . . . includes liability coverage.

Health Insurance [U.S.]

Health-care coverage is available from several government agencies, private carriers, and various types of organizations, such as HMOs.

Medicare [1]

A health plan administered by the federal government to help persons age 65 and over, and others receiving monthly social security disability benefits, meet their health-care costs, [consisting of two parts]:

- Basic Hospital Insurance
  Under the basic hospital insurance coverage of Medicare, commonly called *Part A*, inpatient hospital services . . . are included [for a specified number of days] . . . as well as . . . stays for limited periods in post-hospital extended-care facilities such as nursing homes providing *skilled care*.

- Supplementary Medical Insurance (SMI)
  A voluntary program under Medicare (commonly called *Part B*), provides payment for extra services, such as physicians' and surgeons' services, home health service, X-ray and laboratory services, and counseling services, and requires payment of premiums by participants.

Blue Cross/Blue Shield Plans [1]

Nonprofit prepaid expense plans providing for hospital and surgical medical services, rendered to plan participants by member hospitals and physicians, respectively.

Fee-for-Service or Traditional Indemnity Plan [2]

An insurance plan that provides reimbursement for all or part of your medical expenditures. In general, gives a good deal of freedom to choose your doctor and hospital.

Managed Health Care or Prepaid Care Plan (2)

An insurance plan that entitles you to the health care of a specified group of participating doctors, hospitals, and clinics. These plans are generally offered by health maintenance organizations (HMOs) or variations of them. There are two basic types of managed health care:

- Health Maintenance Organizations (HMOs)
  A prepaid insurance plan that entitles members to the services of participating doctors, hospitals, and clinics. There are three basic types of HMOs:

  Individual Practice Association Plan (IPA)
  An HMO made up of independent doctors, in which the patients visit the doctors and receive their medical treatment in the doctors' regular offices.

  Group Practice Plan
  An insurance plan in which doctors are generally employed directly by an HMO, and members of the HMO must receive their medical treatment from these doctors at a central facility.

  Point-of-Service Plan (POS)
  An insurance plan that allows its members to seek medical treatment from both HMO-affiliated doctors and non-HMO-affiliated doctors.

- Preferred Provider Organization (PPO)
  An insurance plan under which an employer or insurer negotiates with a group of doctors and hospitals to provide health care for its employees or members at reduced rates.

Group versus Individual Health Insurance (2)

Group health insurance refers to the way the health insurance is sold rather than to the characteristics of the insurance policy. Group health insurance is provided to a specific group of individuals who are associated for some purpose other than to buy insurance (for example, as employees of the same company). An *individual insurance policy* is one that is tailor-made for an individual, reflecting age, health (as determined by an examination), geographic location, and chosen deductible amount. Individual policies are expensive, so you should always try to get group insurance.

Other Types of Health Insurance (2)

Other types of health insurance include

- Workers' Compensation
  State laws that provide payment for work-related injuries.

- Medicaid
  A government medical insurance plan for the needy (aged, blind, disabled, and needy families with dependent children). It's a joint program operated by the federal and state governments, with the benefits varying from state to state.

- Medigap Insurance
  Insurance sold by private insurance companies and aimed at bridging gaps in Medicare coverage.

HELP LINE

Canada has national health insurance, funded through taxes, that guarantees universal, comprehensive care to everyone. The only people who opt out of the system are those with the resources and desire to seek more timely care from private providers within Canada or outside its borders. However, Canadians are debating the issue of privatization of health care. A special report in the April 3, 2000, issue of *Maclean's* says:

> Frequently lost in the uproar . . . is the fact that private, for-profit providers already play a large role in the Canadian medical system. Most physicians are private providers who contract their services to the government. Private clinics provide numerous public services ranging from blood tests to radiology and dialysis. The Canadian Institute for Health Information estimates that more than $26 billion of the $86 billion in total health-care spending last year came from private sources (such as individuals and employers)—paying for drugs and dental care, among other services. The question is not whether there should be privatization—but how much further Canadians want to go in that direction.
>
> —Mary Janigan, "Stretching the Medicare Envelope," *Maclean's*, April 3, 2000, p. 48.

Life Insurance (1)

The overriding purpose of life insurance is to protect your family from financial loss in the event of your untimely death. In addition, some types of life insurance also possess attractive investment attributes. Generally, most families can effectively satisfy their insurance needs through the use of one of the three basic types of life insurance: term life, whole life, or universal life. . . . There are . . . other types of life insurance . . . but . . . most of these are simply modifications of these three types.

Term Life Insurance

Insurance that provides only death benefits, for a specified period of time (typically five years), and does not provide for the accumulation of any cash values.

Whole Life Insurance

Life insurance that is designed to offer financial protection for the entire life of the insured; allows for the accumulation of cash values, along with providing stipulated death benefits.

Universal Life Insurance

A type of insurance contract that combines term insurance (death benefits) with a tax-deferred savings/investment account that pays competitive money market interest rates.

Social Security Survivor's Benefits [U.S.]

Benefits included in the social insurance provision of the social security system that are intended to provide basic support for families who have lost their principal wage earners.

—(1) Excerpted from Lawrence J. Gitman and Michael D. Joehnk, *Personal Financial Planning,* The Dryden Press, © 1993, pp. 361, 373, 377, 379, 385, 429-431, 435, 453-459, 461-463, 465. Reprinted by permission of the publisher.

—(2) Excerpted from Arthur J. Keown, *Personal Finance: Turning Money into Wealth,* Prentice-Hall, Inc., © 1998, pp. 322-330. Reprinted by permission of Prentice-Hall, Inc., Upper Saddle River, NJ.

The Cost of Home Ownership

When evaluating the cost of home ownership, consider the following factors.

Down Payment

A portion of the full purchase price provided by the purchaser at the time of purchase of a house or other majorf asset; often called *equity*.

Mortgage Points

Fees (each point equals one percent of the amount borrowed) charged by lenders at the time they grant a mortgage loan; they are related to the lender's supply of loanable funds and the demand for mortgages.

Closing Costs

All expenses (including mortgage points) that borrowers ordinarily pay at the time a mortgage loan is closed and title to the purchased property is conveyed to them. Closing costs are made up of such items as loan application fees, loan origination fees, points (if any), title search and insurance, attorneys' fees, appraisal fees, and other miscellaneous fees for things like mortgage taxes, filing fees, inspections, credit reports, and so on. Closing costs—most of which must be paid by the *buyer*—can amount to several thousand dollars and often total an amount equal to 50 percent or more of the down payment.

Mortgage Payments

For most of the life of a mortgage loan, the vast majority of each monthly payment goes to interest and only a small portion goes toward principal repayment. . . . Mortgage payments often include property tax and insurance payments . . . paid into an *escrow account*. . . . Then . . . the lending institution draws funds from this account to pay required property taxes and homeowner's insurance premiums. Increases in tax rates and/or insurance premiums are passed on to the home buyer in the form of higher monthly loan payments.

■ **PITI**

Notation used to refer to a mortgage payment that includes stipulated portions of *principal*, *interest*, property *taxes*, and homeowner's *insurance*.

■ **Property Taxes**

Taxes levied by local governments on the assessed value of real estate for the purpose of funding schools, law enforcement, and other local services.

■ **Homeowner's Insurance**

Insurance required by mortgage lenders that typically covers the replacement value of a home and its contents.

Maintenance and Operating Expenses

Maintenance costs . . . painting, mechanical repairs, leak repairs, and lawn maintenance, for example, are inescapable facts of homeownership. . . . The cost of utilities, such as electricity, gas, water, and sewage . . . represents a sizable component of homeownership costs.

—Abstracted from Lawrence J. Gitman and Michael D. Joehnk,
Personal and Financial Planning, The Dryden Press, © 1993, pp. 217-223.
Reprinted by permission of the publisher.

Notepad

For families who are having trouble raising a down payment for a home, Arthur J. Keown, Professor of Finance, Virginia Polytechnic Institute and State University, suggests:

If all else fails, consider **Private Mortgage Insurance.** This type of insurance protects the lender in the event that the borrower is unable to make the mortgage payments. This insurance is paid for by the borrower and generally runs from 0.3 percent to 2.0 percent of the loan amount, depending on the down payment level. With private mortgage insurance, many lenders will allow you to borrow more than 80 percent of the appraised value of the home.

—Arthur J. Keown,
Personal Finance: Turning Money into Wealth, Prentice Hall, Inc., 1998, p. 260. Used by permission of Prentice-Hall, Inc., Upper Saddle River, NJ.

Some Investment Options

Investments are assets like stocks, bonds, and mutual funds that are acquired for the purpose of earning a return rather than providing a service. Given that you have adequate savings and insurance to cover any emergencies, the most frequent investment objectives are to

- enhance current income.
- save for a major purchase.
- accumulate funds for retirement.
- seek shelter from taxes [1].

Common Stock

Common stock is basically a form of *equity*—it represents ownership in a corporation [1].

Common Stock Classisfications [2]
- Blue-Chip Stocks
  Common stocks issued by large, nationally known companies with sound financial histories of solid dividend and growth records.

- Growth Stocks
  Common stocks issued by companies that have exhibited sales and earnings growth well above their industry average. Generally these are smaller stocks, and many times they are newly formed companies.

- Income Stocks
  Common stocks issued by mature firms that pay relatively high dividends, with little increase in earnings.

Preferred Stock [2]

Stock that offers no ownership or voting rights and generally pays fixed dividends. The dividends on preferred stock are paid out before dividends on common stock can be issued. It has many of the characteristics of both common stock and bonds.

Bonds [2]

A bond is simply a loan, or an IOU. . . . When you buy a bond, you become a lender. The bond issuer—generally a corporation, the federal government and its agencies, a city, or a state—gets the use of your money and in return pays you interest, generally every six months, for the life of the bond. At maturity, the issuer returns your money, or actually returns the face value of the bond, which may be more or less than what you originally paid for the bond.

Corporate Bonds
Bonds issued by corporations . . . in denominations of $1000 in order to appeal to small investors.

Government Bonds

Without question, the biggest single player—and payer—in the bond market is the U.S. government. There are a number of different types of government debt to choose from:

- Treasury-Indexed Bonds
  Bonds that pay investors an interest rate that's allowed to vary and is set at approximately three percent above the rate of inflation.

- U.S. Series EE Bonds
  Bonds issued by the Treasury with variable interest rates and denominations so low that they can be purchased for as little as $25 each. When a Series EE bond is purchased, its price is one-half its face value, with face values going from $50 to $10,000. . . . You buy a bond, wait a specified amount of time, and get double your money back. They are liquid in the sense that they can be cashed at any time, although cashing them before they mature may result in a reduced yield.

- Agency Bonds
  Bonds issued by government agencies, other than the Treasury, such as the Federal National Mortgage Association (FNMA) and the Federal Home Loan Banks (FHLB).

Municipal Bonds

Bonds issued by states, counties, and cities, as well as other public agencies, such as school districts and highway authorities, to fund public projects.

Mutual Funds [2]

An investment fund that raises funds from investors, pools the money, and invests it in stocks, bonds, and other investments. Each investor owns a share of the fund proportionate to the amount of his or investment. There are various mutual fund classifications.

Money Market Mutual Funds

Mutual funds that invest in Treasury bills, certificates of deposit, commercial paper, and other short-term notes, generally with a maturity of less than 30 days.

Stock Funds

Mutual funds that invest primarily in common stock. Because the stock market is so varied and wide-ranging . . . there are . . . many different types of stock funds to choose from. [A financial planner or broker can provide a description of specific funds and a history of the fund's performance over time.]

Bond Funds

Mutual funds that invest primarily in bonds. Bond funds appeal to investors who want to invest in bonds but don't have enough money to adequately diversify. In general, bond funds emphasize income over growth. Although they tend to be less volatile than stock funds, bond funds fluctuate in value as market interest rates move up and down.

Employer-Sponsored Retirement Plans (2)

Twenty years ago a "guaranteed" pension provided by your employer was the norm. . . . In today's job scene, . . . pension plans are rare. [Instead, employees may participate in a variety of] tax-deferred employer-sponsored retirement plans.

Defined-Contribution Plan

A plan in which you and your employer or your employer alone contributes directly to a retirement account set aside specifically for you . . . a savings account for retirement.

Profit-Sharing Plan

A plan in which the company's contributions vary from year to year depending upon the firm's performance. The amount of money contributed to each employee depends upon the employee's salary level.

Money Purchase Plan

A plan in which the employer contributes a set percent of employees' salaries to their retirement plans annually.

Employee Stock Ownership Plan (ESOP)

A retirement plan in which the retirement benefits are invested directly in the company's stock.

401(k) Plan

A retirement plan in which both the employee's contributions to the plan and the earnings on those contributions are tax-deductible, with all taxes being deferred until retirement withdrawals are made.

403(b) Plan

A tax-deferred retirement plan that's essentially the same as a 401(k) plan except that it's aimed at employees of schools and charitable organizations.

Individual Retirement Funds (2)

Several plans are available for self-employed and small business employees.

Keogh Plan

A tax-sheltered retirement plan for the self-employed.

Self-Employed Pension Plan (SEP-IRA)

A tax-sheltered (you don't pay taxes on any earnings while they remain in the plan) retirement plan aimed at small businesses or at the self-employed. It works like a 401(k) plan, allowing employers to contribute up to 15 percent of the employee's earnings in the SEP, up to a total of $30,000 annually, with the employer contribution going directly into the employee's IRA.

Savings Incentive Match Plan for Employees (SIMPLE)

A tax-sheltered retirement plan aimed at small businesses or the self-employed that provides for some matching funds by the employer to be deposited in your retirement account.

Individual Retirement Account (IRA)

A retirement account to which an individual can contribute up to $2000 annually. This contribution may or may not be tax-deductible depending on the individual's income level and whether he or she or his or her spouse is covered by a company retirement plan.

Roth IRA

An IRA in which contributions are not tax deductible . . . but once the money is in [the fund], it grows tax-free and when it is withdrawn, the withdrawals are tax-free.

Education IRA

An IRA that works just like the Roth IRA, except with respect to contributions. Contributions are limited to $500 annually per child for each child younger than 18, with the income limits beginning at $95,000 for single taxpayers and $150,000 for couples. The earnings are tax-free, and there is no tax on withdrawals made to pay for education.

—(1) Excerpted from Lawrence J. Gitman and Michael D. Joehnk,
Personal Financial Planning, The Dryden Press, © 1993,
pp. 53, 495. Reprinted by permission of the publisher.

—(2) Excerpted from Arthur J. Keown, *Personal Finance: Turning Money into Wealth,*
Prentice-Hall, Inc., © 1998, pp. 452, 476-481, 496, 507, 516, 520, 547, 556-560.
Reprinted by permission of Prentice-Hall Inc., Upper Saddle River, NJ.

Optional Session Plan: Investment Clubs

Session Focus

Investment clubs extend the goal of building wealth to the family and community.

Session Goals

Participants will

- understand how to organize an investment club.
- describe the benefits and risks involved in investing through a club.

HELP LINE

We have not included several components of the session plan (Session Brief, For the Leader, Building Community, and Spiritual Reflection) as we've done for the sessions in the main part of the program guide. Instead, we've only provided a brief outline of content for this session; you'll want to determine how best to present this information and what specific application activities interested participants will need.

Questions People Ask About Investment Clubs

What is an investment club?

An investment club is a group of individuals formed as a legal partnership or corporation.

Why would one consider participating in an investment club?

Three reasons might convince a person to join:

- to grow spiritually (to learn what the Bible says about money).
- to become educated (to learn about investing and the economy).
- to increase wealth (to build financial assets for the future).

Who makes investment decisions in the investment club?

Decision-making involves two steps:

- members research and discuss possible investments.
- club members vote to make final investment decisions.

How do I know how much money I own in the investment club?

Record keeping consists of two parts:

- an accounting system (probably a computer program) tracks member contributions, investments, and the value of a member's investment.

- the club treasurer provides each member with a monthly report of his or her investment.

How safe is my money?
When evaluating safety, remember that

- all investments involve some degree of risk.
- investments in stocks and mutual funds can provide a higher return over the long-term when compared to savings accounts and certificates of deposit.
- investments in stocks and bonds can serve as a protection against inflation over the long term.

What can be done with investments in the investment club?
As wealth accumulates

- profits can be reinvested to make more profits.
- members can withdraw money for family needs and to meet goals.

How are clubs protected from criminal activities?
Club members will want to consider purchasing bonding insurance. Bonding insurance protects the club from theft or negligence in handling the club's money on the part of the club's officers.

How much money do I need to get started?
Each club decides member contributions. For example,

- many clubs require a $20 to $50 contribution per month per member.
- some clubs require as little as $5 to $10 per month per member.

If I'm not ready or able to form or join an investment club, are there other ways to get some of the same benefits?
Mutual funds can produce many of the same benefits.

Bibliography

Bergman, Susan. "The List." *Prism.* May/June, 1998, p. 8.

Blomberg, Craig L. *Neither Poverty Nor Riches.* Grand Rapids, MI: Eerdmans, 1999.

Braver, David. "Wheel Estate." *Utne Reader.* July-August, 1999, p. 21.

Buchanan, Mark. "Trapped in the Cult of the Next Thing." *Christianity Today.* September 6, 1999, p. 66.

Budd, Ken. "Small Change Is Big Money." *Modern Maturity.* July/August, 2000, p. 50.

Building a Better Credit Rating. Washington, D.C.: Federal Trade Commission, 1999.

Carlucci, Alex. "Am I Ready to Own a Home?" (unpublished). Chicago: Prism Mortgage Co., presentation February, 2000.

Chan, Karen, Vicki Fitzsimmons, Rhonda Hardy, Maxine Kimmel, Sondra Stiles, Susan Taylor. *All My Money.* Champaign, IL: University of Illinois Cooperative Extension Service, 1997.

Chan, Karen, "What's My Risk?" (unpublished). Champaign, IL: University of Illinois Cooperative Extension Service, presentations 1999.

Conwell, Russell H. "The History of Fifty-Seven Cents." *The Temple Review.* December 19, 1912. Philidelphia: Convellana-Templana Collection, University Archives, Temple University Library, August, 1997.

Coping with a Credit Crisis. Chicago: Consumer Credit Counseling Services.

Costas, Orlando. *Christ Outside the Gate.* Orbis Books, 1982.

Credit Card Smarts. Champaign, IL: University of Illinois Cooperative Extension Service, 1998.

Crenshaw, Albert B. "Before Risking the Money, Invest in Financial Literacy." *The Washington Post.* May 19, 1996, p. H1.

Davidson, D. Kirk. "Targeting Is Innocent Until It Exploits the Vulnerable." *Marketing News.* September 11, 1995.

Deacon, Ruth, and Francille M. Firebaugh. *Family Resource Management: Principles and Application.* 2nd edition. Boston: Allyn and Bacon, Inc., 1988.

"Dear Consumer" letter. Allen, TX: Experian Information Solutions, Inc., 1999.

"Declaration of Financial Empowerment." *Black Enterprise.* January, 2000, p. 60.

Doheny, Kathleen. "Something Old, Something New." *The Grand Rapids Press.* November 25, 1999, p. B17.

Dugas, Christine. "Bankruptcy Judge Fears Reform Will Hurt Poor the Most." *USA Today.* June 3, 1999, p. 05B.

Dugas, Christine. "Women Rank 1st in Bankruptcy Filings." *USA Today.* June 21, 1999, p. 01A.

Durant, Will. *The Story of Civilization 1: Our Oriental Heritage.* © 1935 by Will Durant, renewed 1963 by Will Durant. New York: Simon & Schuster, 1954.

Easterbrook, Gregg. "Faith Healing—Is Religion Good for You?" *The New Republic.* July 19, 1999, p. 20.

Facts for Consumers. Washington, D.C.: Federal Trade Commission.

Fadiman, Clifton, editor. *The Little, Brown Book of Anecdotes.* New York: Little, Brown and Company, 1985.

Fisher, Christy. "City Lights Beckon to Business." *American Demographics.* October, 1997, pp. 45-46.

For the Common Good. The Council of Michigan Foundations (www.msu.edu/~k12phil).

"Gambling with the Enemy." *Christianity Today.* May 18, 1998, p. 24.

"Generous Donor, 91." *Grand Rapids Press.* September 28, 1999.

Gibran, Kahlil, Martin L. Wolf, Andrew Dib Sherfan, editors; Anthony Rizcallah Ferris, translator. *The Treasured Writings of Kahlil Gibran.* Edison: NJ: Castle Books, 1998.

Gitman, Lawrence J., and Michael D. Joehnk. *Personal Financial Planning.* Fort Worth, TX: The Dryden Press, 1993.

Hardy, Rhonda. "Thrifty Tips." (unpublished). Champaign, IL: University of Illinois Cooperative Extension Service, presentation 1999.

Hobson, Melody. "Long-term Investment Performance (1926-1998)." (unpublished). Chicago: Ariel Capital Management, Inc., presentation December 18, 1999.

Hobson, Melody. "Take $1000 . . ." (unpublished). Chicago: Ariel Capital Management, Inc., presentation December 18, 1999.

Jacoby, Susan. "The Allure of Money." *Modern Maturity.* July/August, 2000, pp. 34, 36-39.

Janigan, Mary. "The Wealth Gap." *Maclean's.* August 28, 2000, p. 46.

Journal of Gerontology: Psychological Studies. 1998, p. S118.

Keown, Arthur J. *Personal Finance: Turning Money into Wealth.* Upper Saddle River, NJ: Prentice-Hall, Inc., 1998.

Knapp, Lee. "Shopping for the Real Me." *Christianity Today.* November 15, 1999, p. 70.

Malveaux, Julianne. "Banking on Us—the State of Black Wealth." *Essence.* October, 1998.

Melton, Joe. "Willy and Ethel" (cartoon). Orlando, FL: North American Syndicate, 1999.

Merriam Webster's Collegiate Dictionary. 10th edition. Springfield, MA: Merriam Webster, Inc., 1995.

Miringoff, Marc, and Marque-Luisa Miringoff. *The Social Health of the Nation.* New York: Oxford University Press, 1999.

Muwakki, Salim, "Wealth Gap Prompts Growing Concern." *Chicago Tribune.* February 14, 2000, p. 15.

Ogilvie, Lloyd J. *Making Stress Work for You.* Dallas: Word Books, 1984.

Oliver, Melvin L., and Thomas M. Shapiro. *Black Wealth/White Wealth.* New York: Routledge, 1997.

"$1 Trillion Racked Up on Plastic." Associated Press, February 25, 1997.

Opening Minds, Changing Lives. Grand Rapids, MI: Open Door Ministries (CRC Publications).

Ortberg, John. *The Life You've Always Wanted.* Grand Rapids, MI: Zondervan Publishing House, 1997.

O'Toole, Patricia. *Money and Morals in America.* New York: Clarkson Potter Publishers, 1998.

Our World Belongs to God: A Contemporary Testimony. Study Version. Grand Rapids, MI: CRC Publications, 1987.

Parker, Star, with Pamela Pearson Wong. "Breaking the Bonds." *Family Voice.* March/April, 2000, p 11.

Pvenke, Maria. "Another Boom Year for Home Building. More Minorities Buying, But Disparities Continue." *USA Today.* June 21, 1999, p. 03A.

Quinn, Jane Bryant. "Home Builders Adjusting As Costs Build." *Chicago Tribune.* April 26, 2000, p. 5-3.

Rand, Ayn. "What Is Capitalism." *The Ayn Rand Reader.* New York: Plume, 1999.

Rice, Gail. "Easy-Reading Scripture Versions." © 1999, Gail Rice.

Sennett, Richard. *The Corrosion of Character: The Personal Consequences of Work in the New Capitalism.* New York: W.W. Norton Company, 1998.

"Sick to Debt!" *McCalls.* June, 2000, p. 65.

Shore, Bill. *Revolution of the Heart.* New York: Riverhead Books, 1995.

Sider, Ronald J. *Just Generosity: A New Vision for Overcoming Poverty in America.* Grand Rapids, MI: Baker Books, 1999.

Stocks, Bonds, Bills and Inflation, 1999 Yearbook. Chicago: Ariel Capital Management, Inc.

Timmer, John. "Half a Century Ago." *The Banner.* May 7, 1990, pp. 10-11.

Universal Savings Accounts—A Route to National Economic Growth and Family Economic Security. Washington, D.C.: Corporation for Enterprise Development (CFED), 1996.

Van Lopik, Susan Weaver. *Just Generosity: A Study and Action Guide.* Grand Rapids, MI: CRC Publications, 1999.

Wolfson, Michael, and Brian Murphy. "Struggle to Pay Rent." *The Toronto Star.* November 6, 1999, p. A1.

Wuorenma, Ruth. "Why I Want to Own a Home." (unpublished). Chicago: Neighborhood Capital Company LLC, presentation November, 1999.

About the Publishers

This program was developed by the MidAmerica Leadership Foundation as it implemented a Community and Economic Development (CED) strategy to revitalize the lives of individuals and communities in Chicago. It is a copublication of MidAmerica Leadership Foundation and CRC Publications.

MidAmerica Leadership Foundation

Based in Chicago, this faith-based organization celebrates God's presence in the city by joining God's mission for justice. In this effort, MLF links congregations and parachurch organizations as well as civic and business leadership.

To that end, MidAmerica Leadership Foundation aims to

- promote *organizational development* that fosters discussion and action between organizations and leaders about issues related to poverty, justice, and diversity.
- empower leaders and organizations—generally faith-based programs or those that contribute to community and economic development—with knowledge, skills, and administrative support to turn their visions into self-sustaining ministries.
- actively build connections between diverse groups, fostering cooperation for everyone's mutual benefit.
- measure results by increases in individual and community assets, knowledge, and affiliations.

For more information about MLF, contact

MidAmerica Leadership Foundation
1111 North Wells, Suite 501
Chicago, IL 60610
Phone: 312-322-3000
Website: www.midamericaleaders.org

CRC Publications

CRC Publications is the publishing ministry of the Christian Reformed Church in North America. It serves the broader Christian community with a wide range of resources offering a biblically Reformed understanding of Scripture. CRC Publications provides

- church education curriculum for all ages,
- discussion and activity materials for youth groups,
- worship and evangelistic resources for churches,
- ministry development and training materials for church leaders,
- inspirational and study materials for families and individuals.

For more information or to obtain a catalog, contact

CRC Publications
2850 Kalamazoo Ave. SE
Grand Rapids, MI 49560-0600
Phone: 1-800-333-8300
Website: www.crcpublications.org
E-mail: editors@crcpublications.org